The Coming of the King

Joe T. Odle

BROADMAN PRESS
Nashville, Tennessee

DEDICATED

To

My Mother and My Sister

Who Share with Me

in the

Glorious Hope

of

The Coming King

4219-26
ISBN: 0-8054-1926-8

Dewey Decimal Classification Number: 236
Library of Congress Catalog Card Number: 73-91612
Printed in the United States of America

Contents

Introduction

Foreword

1. A Book of Prophecy 13

2. Hopeless, Yet There Is Hope 29

3. In The Twinkling of An Eye 43

4. The World's Most Terrible "Week" 61

5. Millennium and After 82

6. The Budding of the Trees 99

7. Getting Ready for the Lord's Return 117

INTRODUCTION

I have read many books and reviewed a number of manuscripts which deal with the second coming of Christ to this earth. But of all I have read, this book, *The Coming of the King,* is best.

This book is superiorly superlative and superlatively superior in the truths and facts it declares — most informative and interesting from the first chapter to the plea in the last chapter.

The author shows how many people are concerned about what is ahead — as shown by their dealing in occultism and horoscopes and fortune tellers. He shows that all men need to know about what is ahead as found in the Bible — the miracle Book of diversity in unity, of harmony in infinite complexity. The Bible is an amazing Book of prophecy — written by holy men of God who spake and wrote as they were moved by the Holy Spirit.

The Bible, inexhaustive in its adequacy, immeasureable in its influence, divinely inspired in totality, is a Book of prophecies fulfilled as to the past and giving prophecies as to the future that will be fulfilled — literally.

In these times of turmoil, tensions, despair, and apostasy, the author sets forth Jesus as the only Way from despair to hope, from darkness to light, from folly to wisdom, from sin to salvation, from strife to peace, from storm to calm.

This book is an invaluable mine of information about

the second coming of Jesus and other realities people need to know. This book merits the reading and study of millions of people. How true are the author's own words: "Just as all the prophecies concerning Christ's first coming were fulfilled literally, there is every reason to believe that all the prophecies that relate to the second coming will be fulfilled just as completely and just as perfectly."

Giving many signs of Christ's second coming, the author has written a book which, as to the second coming and as to men being ready for the imminent return, opens alleys into endless highways of wisdom.

Strong adjectives cannot fully describe the worth of this book to all who need and want to know more of that blessed hope — the second coming of our Lord Jesus. No preacher, no teacher, no Christian ought to be without this masterpiece of thought and wisdom.

ROBERT G. LEE, D.D.
Pastor Emeritus, Bellevue Baptist Church
Memphis, Tenn.

FOREWORD

The world is looking for a king!

Many in America would deny this! We believe in democracy! Yet, some, even in America, seeing the disturbing situation which now confronts the whole world, would be willing to look to a world leader, whether he be called king or president, who could move us out of the present chaos, into a period of peace and prosperity.

Is there a king who can do this? Prophetic Scripture reveals that world governments will turn their power over to such a leader, when the situation becomes too desperate. Both Daniel and Revelation tell about kings who will give their power to a certain king, at a future time. In one of the chapters of this book we shall consider that act, and that king, but he is not the subject of the book. As we begin this series we are thinking of another king . . . a king who is above all other kings . . . a king provided by God himself.

Who is this coming king? Can we know about him? Yes, we do know about him, for we have a book about him . . . a book which tells of his coming and the events which will accompany it.

This King is the Lord Jesus Christ.

Listen to these words of Paul: "I charge thee in the sight of God, who quickeneth all things, and before Jesus Christ . . . that thou keep this commandment without spot, unrebukeable, until the appearing of our Lord Jesus Christ: which in his times he shall shew, who is the blessed and only Potentate, the King of kings, and the Lord of lords; who only hath immortality, dwelling in the light which no man can approach unto; whom no man hath seen, nor can see: to whom be honor and power everlasting. Amen" (1 Tim. 6:13-16).

Pilate asked Jesus, "Art thou the king of the Jews?" And Jesus answered him, "Thou sayest that I am a king. To this end was I born, and for this cause came I unto the world, that I should bear witness unto the truth" (John 18:37).

Over the cross the Romans placed the words, "Jesus of Nazareth, the King of the Jews" (John 19:19). The Jews rejected him, but he was their God-appointed King.

In Revelation 1:5 we read, "Jesus Christ, who is the faithful witness, and the first begotten of the dead, and the prince of the Kings of the earth."

And in Revelation 11:15 "The kingdoms of this earth are become the kingdoms of our Lord, and of his Christ, and he shall reign forever and forever."

Finally consider Revelation 19:16 "And he has on his vesture and on his thigh a name written, King of kings and Lord of lords."

"King of kings and Lord of lords." "To this end was I born, and for this cause came I into the world." "King of the Jews"; "Prince of the kings of the earth"; "the kingdoms of this earth. . . ."

All of these, along with many more passages, reveal a coming kingdom, and a coming King.

That king is the Lord Jesus Christ. His coming is the world's greatest coming event. We call it the second coming of Christ.

We shall study about it in these pages.

To those who accept the Bible as the inspired Word of God, nothing is more certain in the prophetic picture than the second coming of Christ. The person who does not believe in this must acknowledge that he does not believe the Bible, for nothing is more clearly taught than that Christ *is* coming again. Hundreds of passages in both the Old and the New Testament predict the second coming. Bible believers may disagree about the details of events related to the Lord's return, but they cannot disagree on the fact of the return itself.

Many books on the second coming have appeared in the past few years, and it would seem that another hardly is necessary. Dozens of writers have dealt with almost every possible facet of biblical revelation concerning the Lord's return and some of the books have had phenomenal sale. Perhaps there never has been a more widespread interest in the doctrine. As one reads some of the books, however, he has the impression that some of the writers may be going too much into detail, and may be losing most of their readers in the mass of materials which they have assembled. Others deal with certain aspects, but make no effort to cover the whole picture.

This book which you hold in your hand was born out of an invitation for the writer to participate in a Bible Conference, in which he was asked to present a series of messages, which would cover the whole prophetic picture, and which would introduce the average church member to the central truths of the Lord's coming. Preparation for this conference led to long and careful restudy of the whole prophetic message of the Bible, and to an earnest effort so to present eschatological truth that the average Bible student and church member could understand it.

The task of including the whole prophetic message in a few sermons proved to be almost overwhelming, and to present it so that the person who knew little or nothing about prophecy could grasp it was a staggering task. Nevertheless, the Spirit of the Lord gave his blessing and the messages were prepared. What resulted might be called a primer on Bible truth concerning the second coming of Christ.

The author accepts the premillennial interpretation of the Lord's coming. This does not mean that I accept everything taught by some premillennialists. Nevertheless, despite the mistreatment of the doctrine by some, I have found no other interpretation which satisfies my understanding of what the Scripture teaches, or that, in my thinking, can be harmonized with all that the Scriptures teach. These chapters simply seek to present the glorious truths concerning the Lord's return as I have found them in my study of the Word of God.

I would make clear that I have no desire to be dogmatic in my position. I may be mistaken. With all sincerity, however, I have tried to "search the scriptures," allowing them to say that they do say, and then have sought to interpret individual areas in the light of the whole revelation. If I am mistaken, I am sure the Lord will reveal it to me at his coming.

Those who read these pages are urged to recognize that the second coming is only one part of the glorious revelation concerning Jesus Christ, and is only one of numerous important Bible doctrines. Some who study this truth seem to have a tendency to make it their one topic of interest. This is an error.

The second coming of Christ is a very important doctrine and certainly should not be neglected, but it is only one part of the full revelation our Lord has given in his Word. Careful study should be made of all scriptural truth, and not just this one. Balance is needed if we are to be well-rounded Christians and Bible students.

This volume certainly is not to be thought of as the last word in the prophetic revelation. Neither is it written to provide an in-depth study of all Bible prophecy for the use of scholars. A much larger volume and many more messages than are included in this book are needed for full understanding of all facets of this truth. Rather, these are messages presented much as they were preached to live audiences of Christians in a church congregation. At the speaker's request most of the people had their Bibles in hand, and we simply studied the Bible together. To this speaker the experience was a rewarding one which now has been repeated several times.

It is hoped that you will find these pages helpful in introducing you to a great Bible truth. Do not become disturbed if you find unanswered questions, or if some of the areas are not fully discussed. Remember that our Lord has not given full revelation of all things concerning his coming, but has left some things to be clarified at that time. Remember also that the most important fact is that he is coming, and that we are to be ready.

In these pages we seek honestly to interpret the Scriptures, to look at each one in the light of the whole revelation, and to put them in proper perspective in the light of the whole redemptive plan. If I have been able to bring better understanding of prophetic truth, and have helped create a thirst or hunger for more study of these truths, then I shall be glad.

My own conviction, after long study of the Word, is that we well may be living in the very last days before the Lord returns, and that we should be "watching." If, however, he delays his coming another hundred years or a thousand, and we meet him first in death, we still need to live every day as if it were our last, and we still need to understand the revelation concerning his coming.

The return of our Lord as "Kings of kings and Lord of lords" is called in the Bible "that blessed hope," and John tells us in 1 John 3:3, that "everyone that hath this hope in him purifieth himself, even as he is pure." It is my prayer that these pages may lead men to do just that!

JOE T. ODLE

1
A Book of Prophecy

2 Peter 1:21

A world ruler is soon to appear. He will unite the world in a manner in which it never has been united before. He will appear in the last decades of this century.

This is prophecy!

It is a prediction by one of the most noted seers of our day, Jeane Dixon of Washington, D.C.

The same prediction is found in the Bible.

Whether the vision of the modern prophetess, and the inspired revelation which God gave long ago, relate to the same person, is something which only history can determine.

They may be speaking of the same individual, and still they may not.

Moreover, the vision of the modern prophetess may fail to be fulfilled. The prophecy of the Bible will not fail.

Yet, it is of more than passing interest that the modern day clairvoyant, makes a prediction which in so many ways parallels the long standing prophecy of the Word of God.

In the book *A Gift of Prophecy* by Ruth Montgomery, a story of the life and work of Jeane Dixon, the experience of the coming world ruler vision is related in full detail.

Mrs. Dixon speaks of it as her "most significant and soul stirring vision." In it she saw that there was born somewhere in the Mideast in the early morning hours of February 5, 1962, a child whose life will change world history. She saw that before the end of this century he would bring together men of all races into one all-embracing faith.

The vision revealed that this man's power will begin to be felt in the 1980's, and that in the decade following, evidently under his leadership, the world will move into an era without wars and suffering. His power is to grow greatly until 1999, at which time the world will discover the full meaning of the vision.

The prophecy is of interest to the average person because he is concerned about the future and in what is to take place in the years just ahead. It is of special interest to serious Bible students, because of its similarity to an important prophecy in the Bible.

Multitudes of people listen to Jeane Dixon when she speaks. She gained worldwide prominence in the field of clairvoyance when she predicted the assassination of President Kennedy. Several years prior to Mr. Kennedy's election to the nation's highest office, she predicted in an interview published in a national magazine, that the President elected in 1960 would be killed while in office. As the time for the tragic occurrence approached, her impressions seemed to grow stronger, so that only days before the Dallas rifle shots, she is reported to have begged a friend of the President's to urge him not to make the trip. On the morning of the President's death, sitting at breakfast in a Washington restaurant, she is said to have stated that this is the day that it would happen. She was talking about the shooting of the President. It is no wonder that a person who has the gift for making such predictions has a following of those who listen.

Of course, Jeane Dixon misses on some of her predictions, so that there are skeptics who challenge her claims to a special gift of prophecy. However, so many of them, like this concerning the President, are so uncannily accurate, that only the most stubborn can deny that she has some unusual power.

It is interesting to note, as we consider her prediction of a coming ruler, that this same idea of a world ruler being born on February 5, 1962, is corroborated by others. For months before that date, we are told that astrologers and soothsayers had been saying that an earthshaking event would occur on that day. They claimed that their predictions were based upon a rare conjunction of the planets. Furthermore, in his book *The Coming One,* Dr. Kurt Koch, widely known German Christian lecturer and writer, says that there is a widespread belief in the Middle East today that a child born in 1962 will gain world power before the end of this century, and that he is first to be revealed about 1980.

The Bible sets no dates, but many serious Bible students have found in it a clear prediction of a coming world ruler, who is called in the Bible the Antichrist. He is to be a world figure in the last days of the present age, and plays an important role in world events related to the second coming of Christ. A more complete biblical picture of what he is to be will be presented in a later chapter of this book.

The Bible also presents another world ruler who is yet to come, the Lord Jesus Christ, who is spoken of among other titles, as "King of kings and Lord of lords." Speaking of him the Bible says, "The kingdoms of this world are becoming the kingdoms of our Lord, and of his Christ; and he shall reign for ever and ever." His kingdom is to be from sea to sea, and no power or force will be able to withstand him.

It seems evident that even if the present day "prophets" are speaking of one of these men presented in Bible proph-

ecy, it is of the first one, the Antichrist. There seem to be
no prophecies of one who matches the biblical description
of the coming eternal King.

Since they do make such predictions, it is natural to
ask, "What is the source of the knowledge of these present
day seers?" Their "prophecies" are far different from
those to whom the Lord gave biblical revelations. Bible
prophets do not make predictions which do not come to
pass; modern seers often do. Yet these of our day are
right often enough that it must be acknowledged that they
have some unusual power or gift. Whence does it come?

Consider, for example, Jeane Dixon, whose predictions
have been mentioned. She is a Washington business
woman and housewife, who through her life has appeared
to possess special psychic powers. She is said to use many
channels in receiving her revelations and prophecies, including visions, the crystal ball, astrology, numerology,
dreams, cards, an inner voice, mental telepathy, extrasen-
sory perception (ESP) and finger touching. Through
these she receives her revelatory information.

Currently others apparently possessing such powers in-
clude witches, soothsayers, mystics, astrologers, practi-
tioners of the occult, and others. There is a widespread practice in these fields today.

Since at least some of them apparently have ability to
foretell coming events, many ask concerning the source
of their gift. Is it from God or from Satan? Or is it
merely some unusual natural gift? Some are convinced
that such gifts are demonic, and are a revelation of sa-
tanic activity in the world.

Whatever their source, these strange powers long have
been in existence, for even in the days of Moses the
Israelites were forbidden to have anything to do with them.
Listen to these words from Deuteronomy 18:9-12.

"When thou art come into the land which the Lord thy God giveth thee, thou shalt not learn to do after the abominations of those nations. There shall not be found among you any one that maketh his son or daughter to pass through the fire, or that useth divination, or an observer of times, or an enchanter, or a witch, or a charmer, or a consulter with familiar spirits or a wizard, or a necromancer [one who calls up spirits from the dead]. For all that do these things are an abomination unto the Lord."

From the words of Moses it is evident that many of the practices of our day were commonplace long centuries ago. Any careful student of ancient history knows of the mystical religions of Babylon and of the strange cults of Egypt. Practices of today are not too far different from some of them, and many feel that their source is the same. One is amazed when he finds how widespread the practices are today, and how many are involved in them. Because of this it is of momentous importance to lovers of the Word of God, when some of these modern cultists or seers deal in matters which appear to have some relationship to Bible prophecy.

There is a widespread interest today in what is to happen to our nation and to the world in the immediate future. The world seems to move from one crisis to another, and many are alarmed and distressed at what they see coming to pass. National and international conflict, revolution, population explosion, unbelievable social change, economic crisis, hunger, and other factors, bring confusion and disturbance across the world. Even world leaders and learned men often are quoted as saying that they see no hope for the future. Some have even predicted that civilization will destroy itself, or collapse, before the end of this century. In such a time it is natural that people turn to "prophets" to try to learn what is ahead. Perhaps this explains the apparent surge of practice of such arts today, and the alarming increase of interest in them.

Christians are interested in coming things just as much, or even more, than the rest of the world's people. They not only have the natural concern about world conditions, but also believe that God is running the affairs of the world, and that he has revealed in his Word what he wants his people to know about the future. Christians may be interested in the modern day seers, simply to know what they are saying, but they do not need the wisdom of these "prophets" to know what is coming to pass in the world. In their hands they have a book which already has written down all that God wants man to know about what is coming. He has revealed so much that any careful student of the Bible knows of coming events which this world faces — and the destiny of mankind.

In this book it is our purpose to briefly look at what the Bible says about what is ahead for the world, especially as it relates to the second coming of Christ, which is the greatest coming event in God's purpose for the world. We shall examine many of the coming events which are clearly revealed, and shall try to understand what they mean to us now and in the future. As we see them, we shall understand why the Christian does not need modern clairvoyants or other mystics to give assurance of what is ahead. As one great preacher of the past generation said, "I know my future. It is written down in a book which I have in my hand."

However, before we begin to examine these prophecies of coming events, we first must recognize that the Bible is a prophetic book. Until one understands this it will be difficult for him to comprehend the revelation which God has made concerning future things.

A recent book, *Encyclopedia of Biblical Prophecy*, by J. Barton Payne, lists every prophecy of the Bible, with its fulfillment if that already has occurred. He reveals that there are 737 different prophecies in the Bible. Many of these relate to minor matters, while others are major in their import. Hundreds of the prophecies already have been fulfilled, for they related to events that are now past. Hundreds of others, however, still await fulfilment, for they relate to events yet to come. In the case of those prophecies already fulfilled, one finds that the fulfilment was perfect in every detail, and that the prophets were not mistaken in the slightest particular. There is no reason to believe that biblical prophecies of events yet to come to pass shall be less exact in their accuracy.

Most of the hundreds of Bible prophecies still to be fulfilled relate to the coming of earth's one glorious and eternal king, the Lord Jesus Christ. This is spoken of in the Bible by various terms such as the "return" or "coming" of the Lord, and as the "blessed hope." It is commonly called the second coming of Christ. In this book we shall study many of the particulars of this glorious event, and its meaning to the world.

First, however, we must understand that the Bible is a book of prophecy, and that in it God has revealed the things which are yet to come to pass. This fact of the Bible's prophetic character is well revealed by the apostle Peter in his second epistle. Listen to his words.

In 2 Peter 1:15-18 we read, "Moreover I will endeavour that ye may be able after my decease to have these things always in remembrance. For we have not followed cunningly devised fables, when we made known unto you the power and coming of our Lord Jesus Christ, but were eyewitnesses of his majesty. For he received from God the Father honour and glory, when there came such a voice to him from the excellent glory, This is my beloved Son, in whom I am well pleased. And this voice which came from heaven we heard, when we were with him in the holy mount."

Peter is speaking of the transfiguration, an experience which previewed the glory that Jesus one day was to have. Remembering that experience he says, "We are not following some fable. We are telling you what we saw with our own eyes." In the next verse he continues, "We have also a more sure word of prophecy; whereunto ye do well that ye take heed, as unto a light that shineth in a dark place, until the day dawn, and the day star arise in your hearts: Knowing this first, that no prophecy of the scripture is of any private interpretation. For the prophecy came not in old time by the will of man: but holy men of God spake as they were moved by the Holy Spirit."

This is a wonderful passage of Scripture. Peter begins by saying, "As we presented the message of God unto you we have not presented fables, cunningly devised fables, but we are eyewitnesses of the glory of the Lord." And then he adds, "It is a more sure word of prophecy and ye ought to give heed to it because the prophecy did not come by the will of man, but holy men of God spake as they were moved by the word of God and you have it."

A "Sure Word"

We have God's Word. We do not need the wild guesses of people who may be led by evil spirits. We have a revelation from God that tells us what is ahead. We have the sure word of prophecy.

Immediately someone says, "Wait a minute, preacher. Do you think that the Bible is inspired in a manner not true with other books?" Yes, I believe this book is unusual. "Do you think this book is greater than other litera-

ture?" Yes, I believe this book is greater than other literature. Peter says here that the "prophecy came not in
old time by the will of man: but holy men of God spoke
as they were moved by the Holy Spirit." This book is different because this book is divine. Only God can know the
future and God has spoken through his Word. When you
and I as Christians simply accept the Bible and believe the
Bible, we do not have to worry about the future. We
know what it is going to be, because God has revealed all
of it that we need to know.

Some skeptic may say, "Do you really believe that the
whole Bible is inspired." Yes, I do. He may ask, "Do
you mean that you believe that the Old Testament is
authentic as history?" Yes, it is! I know that there are
those who have attacked it, and that all kinds of charges
are made against it, but I suggest that you challenge those
who make such charges to point out the errors. Challenge
them to bring the charge to a thoroughly trained conserva-
tive scholar and see what happens.

A Book of Prophecy

As we look at the Bible we find that it is filled with
prophecy. What do we mean by prophecy? Prophecy is
foretelling or prediction of what is to come. You and I
cannot foretell the future. I can't tell what is going to
happen tomorrow. I know that commentators and pollsters
predict what is coming, for example, in elections. What
they present may be good guesses because they are based
upon surveys they already have made, but actually they
cannot tell with certainty what is going to happen tomorrow, or next year, or five years from now.

If a man could know what's going to happen in
North Carolina, or Mississippi, or the United States for
the next twelve months — if a man had that knowledge,

he could be a millionaire very quickly simply by selling
his knowledge. But God has not revealed to us what is
going to happen in our lives individually or what is going
to happen in our nation except as it is revealed in his
Word. We cannot deal with specific things and say this is
going to happen or that is going to happen, except as
specific things are revealed in the Word of God.

The Bible is a book of prophecy. There are numerous
whole books of prophecy in the Old Testament and
one full book in the New Testament, but there are many
other prophetic passages throughout the Bible. One of the
proofs that this is the Word of God is that the prophecies
come to pass.

Prophecies to Abraham

In the fifteenth chapter of the book of Genesis, God
gave Abram an astonishing prophecy. This is before
Abram had even been promised his son from whom the
nation of Israel was to be born. But here is a prophecy
made long before it came to pass. Genesis 15:13 says,
"And he said unto Abram, know of a surety that thy seed
shall be a stranger in a land that is not theirs, and shall
serve them; and they shall afflict them four hundred years.
And also that nation, whom they shall serve, will I judge:
and afterward shall they come out with great substance."

Here, long before it came to pass, is a prophecy that
Israel, as a people, was going to be carried into bondage
into Egypt, and that Israel would serve there 400 years
and then would be delivered from that land as God dealt
with that nation in judgment. That prophecy was fulfilled exactly as it was spoken long before.

There were many other similar prophecies. In Genesis
17:16 Abram was told that he was to be the father of
many nations. In Genesis 16:12, Hagar was told that
her son, who was still to be born, would be a wild man,

with his hand against every man. Read the history of
Ishmael and you will find prophecy was fulfilled exactly.
In Genesis 18:10 Abram was told that he would have a
son in his old age and it was fulfilled in Isaac.

God Speaks Through Moses

In Deuteronomy 28 we find one of the most incredible
prophecies in all the Bible. Moses is speaking to the
children of Israel before they go into the Promised Land
to become a nation. He already has told them that as
long as they do God's will they will be blessed; and then
he said something amazing, foretelling their history hundreds and even thousands of years before it happened. This
is one of the proofs that the Bible is the Word of God.

**And it shall come to pass, that as the Lord re-
joiced over you to do you good, and to multiply you;
so the Lord will rejoice over you to destroy you,
and to bring you to nought; and ye shall be plucked
from off the land whither thou goest to possess it.**

**And the Lord shall scatter thee among all people,
from the one end of the earth even unto the other;
and there thou shalt serve other gods, which neither
thou nor thy fathers have known, even wood and
stone.**

**And among these nations shalt thou find no ease,
neither shall the sole of thy foot have rest: but the
Lord shall give thee there a trembling heart, and
failing of eyes, and sorrow of mind:**

**And thy life shall hang in doubt before thee; and
thou shalt fear day and night, and shalt have none
assurance of thy life:**

**In the morning thou shalt say, Would God it were
even! and at even thou shalt say, Would God it were
morning! for the fear of thine heart wherewith thou**

shalt fear, and for the sight of thine eyes which thou shalt see (vv. 63-67).

This is a prophecy concerning Israel. It was made before they were in the Promised Land. Moses was looking ahead hundreds of years to that period when, because of their sins, the people were going to be snatched off this land and were going to be scattered to the four winds of the earth. In those lands God was going to preserve them as a people, but they were going to suffer as no other people ever had suffered.

If you are familiar with the history of the Jews, you know how perfectly this passage was fulfilled. They did go into the land. They lived there several hundred years. Finally, however, they were driven out of the land, first the Northern tribes and then Judah. A part of Judah came back after 70 years exactly as was prophesied by Jeremiah. Most of them, however, never were brought back. They were scattered among the nations. Yet they did not cease to exist, nor have they even until today. This is the most amazing thing. Jews are found in almost every nation around the world. They have not been swallowed up by the other nations. Jews in our land are Americans but they also are Jews.

Now I'm an American. My people came from North Carolina into Indiana and then on to Illinois. I know that there is some Scotch, and some Irish blood in me. But I'm not Scotch or Irish — I'm just American. The Jew is is still a Jew, and though his fathers were scattered to the ends of the earth, and though they have been condemned to die in nation after nation, and though millions of them have been murdered, they have continued to exist as a distinct people. Although some nations took the property away from every Jew, they have lived on. England did that. In Spain an order was given to kill every Jew in the nation. In Nazi concentration camps more than six million of them were killed by Hitler. Yet they have lived on, exactly as Moses said.

But we haven't finished the prophecy. Moses prophesied further. We were reading in chapter 28 where he said "I will scatter you." Now look at 30:1-5.

And it shall come to pass, when all these things are come upon thee, the blessing and the curse, which I have set before thee, and thou shalt call them to mind among all the nations, whither the Lord thy God hath driven thee.

And shalt return unto the Lord thy God, and shalt obey his voice according to all that I command thee this day, thou and thy children, with all thine heart, and with all thy soul;

That then the Lord thy God will turn thy captivity, and have compassion upon thee, and will return and gather thee from all the nations, whither the Lord thy God hath scattered thee.

If any of thine be driven out unto the outmost parts of heaven, from thence will the Lord thy God gather thee, and from thence will he fetch thee:

And the Lord thy God will bring thee into the land which thy fathers possessed, and thou shalt possess it; and he will do thee good, and multiply thee above thy fathers.

Now not all this has been fulfilled. They have not yet been converted. They have not yet fully turned to the Lord, but God has brought them back as a nation to their own land. Ezekiel said it would happen. Isaiah said it would happen. Others said it would happen. Jesus said it would happen, but Moses said it more than 3,000 years ago. The Jews were going to be scattered to the ends of the earth, but one day they would be brought back to their own land. Here is a prophecy that literally has been fulfilled. If you didn't believe the Bible for anything else than this, here is a proof that you need to remember.

Isaiah, Prince of Prophets

Let us look at one other prophecy. We could consider many others. Consider the prophecy of Isaiah concerning the destruction of Babylon. Turn to Isaiah 13:19. "And Babylon, the glory of kingdoms, the beauty of the Chaldees' excellency, shall be as when God overthrew Sodom and Gomorrah. It shall never be inhabited, neither shall it be dwelt in from generation to generation: neither shall the Arabian pitch tent there; neither shall the shepherds make their fold there. But wild beasts of the desert shall lie there: and their houses shall be full of doleful creatures."

That is like saying New York City is going to be a pile of ruin and nobody will dwell there. Babylon was the most glorious city in the world in that day. Yet, God revealed to Isaiah that Babylon was to be destroyed, that it would not be rebuilt, and that the Arabian would not spend the night there, and the wild animals will make their dens there.

Sometime ago I read a report written by a scientist who was doing research in the Middle East. He told of how that, with Arab guides, he made the trip out from a city not too far away, to visit the ruins of this old city of Babylon.

"It was such a fascinating thing to dig and to examine the walls and the ruins of the ancient civilization. When evening came, I was ready to spend the night there in order to continue the work the next day, but I noticed that the Arabs were folding their tents." And he said,

"Wait a minute we're going to spend the night." And they said, "No, no. No Arab ever spends the night in this city. We can't stay here. We go back. You stay if you want to stay. We go back." And they left.

Isaiah had said, "Neither shall the Arabian pitch his tent there. Neither shall it be rebuilt." Here is a prophecy spoken by Isaiah while the great city was the most famous metropolis of the world. But God has said that it would be destroyed and never be rebuilt and that wild animals would make their dens there. That prophecy came true exactly as God's prophet said.

Summary

We could point out numerous other prophecies. Some of them will be considered in later chapters. In the next chapter we shall look at some of the amazing prophecies concerning Jesus Christ. It is most thrilling to see passage after passage gloriously fulfilled. All of this says one thing, "This is God's Word." If all the prophecies of events now past have been fulfilled exactly as the prophet said, can't you and I believe the rest of the prophecies for which fulfillment is yet future? If everything that was said by the prophets concerning the first coming of Christ came to pass exactly as was prophesied, do you and I need to have any questions concerning the rest of those promises?

In his book *Why I Preach That the Bible Is Literally True,* (Broadman Press, p. 30), W. A. Criswell says,

Why do I believe that the Bible is literally true? One cogent reason can be found in the literal fulfilment of its prophecies. The outstanding, differentiating characteristic of Israel's religion is predictive prophecy. Only in the Bible will you find the phenomenon of prophecy.

Where is there a God of Gods? Where is there a founder of religions, such as Confucius, Buddha, Muhammad or Zoroaster; or where is there any other who could with such certainty predict the future? Where is there a statesman who, in these times, can foretell what will be the condition of things in Europe or in America one hundred years from now or even ten years from now? . . . We do not know the future. It is the prerogative of God to know what tomorrow will bring. The fulfilled prophecies of the Bible bespeak the omniscience of its author.

The Bible predicts accurately, clearly the things which are to happen centuries and even millenniums away.

Generations come and go and yet the Word of God lives! Nations rise and fall, yet it lives! Kings, dictators, presidents come and go, but the Word of God lives! Hated, despised, cursed, yet it lives! Doubted, suspected, criticized, yet it lives! Condemned by the atheist, yet it lives! Scoffed by the scorners, exaggerated by fanatics, misconstrued and misstated, ranted and raved about, its inspiration denied, its history smeared, but it just lives on and on! To know it is to love it! To love it is to accept it! To accept it is to find eternal life!

As we begin these studies, we can accept the fact that we do not have to depend on fortune-tellers, or soothsayers, or the stars, or any other such thing. We have the Word of God! We do not know what is ahead of us tomorrow, but we know who holds tomorrow and we know what he has promised in his Word. We can depend on those promises because they never fail. God's Word is a prophetic book.

2
Hopeless, Yet There Is Hope

1 Timothy 6:14

The twentieth century began with all kinds of dreams that this century was going to be the beginning of the millennium. Some great Baptist leaders believed that. Dr. B. H. Carroll, who was a tremendous preacher and an outstanding Bible scholar, evidently believed that this twentieth century was going to be the start of God's millennium. He felt that it was going to be the beginning of the wonderful things which the Bible had prophesied and he wrote that in his commentary on Daniel, and in his commentary on Revelation. They are postmillennial in their view, teaching that Christianity will so change the world that the millennium will come.

Well, World War I began before Dr. Carroll died in 1916. A very close friend of his, Dr. W. H. Horton, who also was a friend of mine, told me that he talked to Dr. Carroll several times after World War I had begun in 1914, and that Dr. Carroll said that he wished he could live long enough to rewrite his commentaries on Revelation and Daniel, because he had been mistaken about the millennium.

There were many men at the beginning of this century who believed that the millennium had begun. One man wrote that science, art, literature, and governments all had come into the train of Jesus Christ, and that the world was about to enter an age without sin. That was the view at the beginning of this century.

Hopeless

Now we are in the seventh decade of that century and we know that it has been the bloodiest century of history. More men have died in war in this century than in any other in all of history. A man has to be an optimist today to believe that civilization will survive the twentieth century.

I have an article clipped from the *National Observer* of March 1972. In it is found a story entitled "Doomsday." This is a report of a conference held at Smithsonian Institution in Washington. This meeting was attended by scientists and scholars of such stature as Wernher Von Braun.

At this meeting a group of young researchers, who had been studying world conditions, said bluntly that unless man repents and changes his habits and life-styles, civilization will reach its growth limits within 100 years and then collapse. Now that wasn't a preacher saying that. That was a group of young scientists. They averaged twenty-six years of age. They said that only disaster faces us unless we change our direction.

The article also says, "There are five factors in our lives: population, industrial output, agricultural production, depletion of natural resources, and pollution." Based on present trends, these studies found that when they fed all the variables into their computers "only disaster came out." Only disaster! Preachers of God's Word reading their Bibles have for a long time said that world conditions are going to get worse and worse. But now, other men are saying it.

Professor Albert Webber, who was a great historian, said in his book *Farewell to European History,* written only a few years ago, "To the one who is endowed with historical perspective it must be clear that we are at the end of world history as we know it."

H. G. Wells, who was an even more widely known historian, said in his book *The Mind At the End of Its Tether*, "I predict that the generation in which you and I live is the last generation upon the earth."

And Arnold J. Toynbee, who is called by many the greatest modern historian, said in the *New York Times* sometime ago, "The stable characteristics of the past 6,000 years of civilized history are being changed and are falling apart."

At a great meeting in London in 1971, a group of the world's scientists, and leaders in other fields of knowledge, were asked the question, "What will be the world's condition in the year 2000?" And unanimously they said, "The world will not be in existence in the year 2000."

Despair! Hopelessness! Men are saying, "What can we do?" We live in a day of the greatest scientific achievements man ever has known, but are they making this a better world? No! They are building instruments so that a man could press a button today and kill everybody in the world within a few hours. I read sometime ago that they now have bombs so terrible that a few of them could be exploded off the coast of California and everything in America would be dead in three days. An article appearing early in 1972 reported that some Americans believe that Russia has some of their hydrogen bombs in the air right now.

Yes, we have made scientific advance. We have moved forward educationally, and have made tremendous progress, yet we are told that in this decade we probably are going to come to such a food crisis that man can no longer feed himself. In the book *Population Explosion,* Paul Erlich, a professor at Stanford University in California, says that by the mid-1970s or at least by the 1980s the United States will have to decide which nations it is going to let starve to death and which nations it is going to keep alive. This is a note of despair. It is not the word of some ranting and raving preacher, but of scientists and world leaders.

I sat on a plane not long ago with a professor from the University of Georgia. He said, "The time is not too far away here in the United States when we will not be able to produce enough food to feed America." My first reaction was that the man was out of his mind, but then I began to read some of the books on what is happening to our ecology.

Even as this book was being prepared for the press, the energy crisis suddenly struck the world. For many years, growing demands of an ever increasing population used up more and more of the resources. A few men had warned that the world was facing trouble in the energy area, but nobody was listening or really believed it. We had been taught that man had become self-sufficient in his technological achievement. In the light of this we erected larger homes, bought bigger cars, raced along the highways at higher speeds, and made increasing demands for electricity and other energy for our homes and businesses.

Then suddenly the energy crisis struck. We learned that this nation, and some others, were running out of oil, out of gas, and out of other energy sources. We were told that we must decrease our speeds, dim our lights, lower our thermostats, and readjust our whole life-style. Gasoline and heating prices began to soar, and limitations were placed on the use of oil in other areas. This brought the probability of upcoming shortages in many products which have become commonplace in our lives. Moreover, it was revealed that there already are shortages in steel, in paper, in fertilizer and even in some food products. Already we had known of the lowering of water levels, with the problems that brought. While it was not a time to panic, we suddenly became aware that a serious crisis confronted us, and that solution was not going to be easy to accomplish. Power play by oil producing nations did not make the situation easier. National leaders moved instantly to seek answers to the crisis, but gave no promise of early solution. One had only to read the newspapers or listen to the radio or television to know that man's self-sufficiency was not as great as most had assumed. The world situation was bad and apparently growing worse.

Is There No Hope?

Jeremiah said, in the eighth chapter, "Is there no balm in Gilead? Is there no physician there?" The world situation, as we look at it from a human point of view, is hopeless and men who are depending upon science and on what man can do are depending upon a broken stick. Despite all of its education, all of its scientific knowledge, all the marvelous things that are being done with the computers, and all other scientific gains which are being made, our world continues to get sicker and sicker.

"Ah, but there is hope! Paul spoke, in our text, of the appearing of Christ . . . who is the blessed and only Potentate, the King of kings and Lord of lords." This is the hope . . . a King is coming . . . and God already has revealed the plans for the "kingdoms of this world" to become his kingdoms. In an hour when the world is facing despair, when men say that we are moving toward disaster, we can reply, "Wait; the King is coming." We do not have to worry about bombs and the threatenings of sinful men. We do not have to fear population explosion or moral collapse. Let Satan do his worst. (Evidently he must be doing that today.)

The moral climate of our nation defies description. When one of the most popular national magazines for women announced that its April 1972 issue was to have a full double spread center section of a male nude, the newsstands said all copies were reserved even before the publication date. When we read that, we can only ask "What has happened to us morally in America?" Yet, even that doesn't upset me, because I can say with Paul, my hope is in Jesus Christ. I have the Bible and I know that God says he has set limitations on what men can do, and how far he is going to let them go. We know what God is going to do because he has revealed it in his Word. God is still running human affairs. When friends said to David, "What can the righteous do when the foundations are destroyed?" he replied, "God is still on his throne. My hope is in the Lord." If you are a Christian, if you are a child of God, you do not have to depend on man's inabilities. Depend on God's glorious abilities. God will still do what he plans to do.

The book of Daniel reveals God's hand in human history. God spoke to King Nebuchadnezzar, through a great dream. This is revealed in Daniel 2:37 in these words: "Thou, O king, art a king of kings: for the God of heaven hath given unto thee a kingdom, power, and strength, and glory." The God of heaven had given unto the king these things. Later in the prophecy Daniel tells of how God will destroy that kingdom. This reveals that men's kingdoms are in God's hands. To know the final outcome of world kingdoms look at Daniel 7:13-14. "I saw in the night visions, and, behold, one like the Son of man came with the clouds of heaven, and came to the Ancient of days, and they brought him near before him. And there was given him dominion, and glory, and a kingdom, that all people, nations, and languages, should serve him."

Here is God giving a human king his power and his place, but in his own time when he is ready, he is going to give his own Son the position of glory and power, and the world will worship him. When we know that God still has the world in his hands, we do not need to be afraid. As we begin to study the Bible, we discover a great fact. In the preceding chapter of this book we saw that the Bible is a prophetic book, and as we read it we find ourselves saying with another, "There's a Man in this Book!" Careful study reveals that that man is the Lord Jesus Christ, the coming King.

The Twofold Picture

Let us look at 1 Peter 1:10-11. Here is a clear statement that Christ is at the center of the biblical message. "Of which salvation the prophets have inquired and searched diligently, who prophesied of the grace that should come unto you: Searching what, or what manner of time the Spirit of Christ which was in them did signify, when it testified beforehand the sufferings of Christ, and the glory that should follow."

Here are two truths concerning Christ. The name "Christ" means "the anointed one." He was God's Chosen One, and Peter says that as we study the prophets we find that they were searching. They wanted to understand what God was saying when he talked about a suffering Christ and also a glorified Christ. "The sufferings of Christ and the glory that should follow."

Hebrews 9:28-29 states "So Christ was once offered to bear the sins of many, and unto them that look for him shall he appear the second time, without sin [that is, no longer to make a sin offering] unto salvation." Here again

we find the suffering of Christ and the glory that should
follow. Christ came first to die, and he is coming again
in glorious exaltation. Here is the picture of Christ that
we find all through the Bible, a suffering Savior and a
reigning king. Let us study further to help us understand
this apparent contradiction.

There is an invisible red line running through the Bible,
which we could call God's redemptive plan. The coming
of Christ was no accident. From the foundation of the
world God planned the whole redemptive program. God
is running this universe!

In the Garden of Eden, in the very beginning of history,
when sin had entered the world, God said to the first
couple in Genesis 3:15, "I will put enmity between thee
and the woman [he is talking to Satan], and between thy
seed and her seed; it shall bruise thy head, and thou shalt
bruise his heel." Here is the promise that the seed of
woman . . . not of man . . . the seed of woman, would
bruise Satan. God would provide victory through the seed
of woman. It was the very first home, the very first family,
yet God, even there, gave his promise of redemption.

In Genesis 12:3 we have another redemptive promise,
"In thee shall all families of the earth be blessed." Most
Bible scholars believe that this is a messianic promise, that
through the seed of Abram is to come the promised Redeemer. In Genesis 49:10 the aged Jacob says, "The
sceptre shall not depart from Judah, nor a lawgiver from
between his feet, until Shiloh come." Here is this old
patriarch somehow foreseeing that God was giving to his
people a deliverer called Shiloh. That was a prophecy,
although perhaps a dim one to him, of a coming redeemer. In Numbers 24:17 Balaam was forced to say
something which he didn't mean to say or want to say
"A Star out of Jacob, and a Sceptre out of Israel." God

was continuing to give the promise — a Redeemer is coming.

Look at Deuteronomy 18 for a moment. These are words of Moses spoken to the children of Israel immediately before they went into the Promised Land. Listen to this promise in the verses 18-19: "I will raise them up a Prophet from among their brethren, like unto thee, and will put my words in his mouth; and he shall speak unto them all that I shall command him. And it shall come to pass, that whosoever will not hearken unto my words which he shall speak in my name, I will require it of him."

God was saying through Moses that one day he would send a prophet — *The Prophet*. That is capitalized in the Bible because it was a word concerning God's prophet . . . God's man who was coming to this earth. Some may say that it has no reference to Jesus. Can they be sure? Note what Jesus says in Luke 24:27: "And beginning at Moses and all the prophets, he expounded unto them in all the scriptures the things concerning himself." Could he have read these very words of Moses here? Who knows?

Moses saw him! Abraham saw him! Jesus said, "Abraham saw my day and rejoiced." They all heard that promise of God that one day a Redeemer is coming. Space does not permit us to look at the marvelous second Psalm which is a prophetic psalm, and the twenty-second Psalm which describes the death of Christ on the cross, and the sixty-eighth Psalm and the sixty-ninth Psalm and others.

We must, however, turn to two or three passages in Isaiah. We could consider whole chapters but we must limit our study to a few passages. We read in Isaiah 2:2: "And it shall come to pass in the last days, that the mountain of the Lord's house shall be established in the top of the mountains, and shall be exalted above the hills;

and all nations shall flow unto it." And Isaiah says, "for out of Zion shall go forth the law and the word of the Lord from Jerusalem" (v. 3).

And here is a ruler, "And he shall judge among the nations, and shall rebuke many people: and they shall beat their swords into plowshares, and their spears into pruninghooks: nation shall not lift up sword against nation, neither shall they learn war any more. O house of Jacob, come ye, and let us walk in the light of the Lord" (vv. 4-5).

This passage tells of a day when a Redeemer is coming. There are many other prophecies of Christ in Isaiah. We know about the seventh chapter and the prediction of the wondrous Son born of a virgin. We know from the ninth chapter about the one who is to be "a son," and "the government is to be on his shoulder"; and he is to be "called Wonderful, Counsellor, The mighty God, The everlasting Father." What a picture this was.

Look at the eleventh chapter of Isaiah. Here is the picture of the son of David — of Jesse and of David, coming — "The spirit of the Lord shall rest upon him, the spirit of wisdom and understanding," and then the prophet says, "The wolf shall dwell with the lamb, and the leopard shall lie down with the kid; and the calf and the young lion and the fathing together; and a little child shall lead them. And the cow and the bear shall feed; their young ones shall lie down together: . . . the sucking child shall play on the hole of the asp, and the weaned child shall put his hand on the cockatrice's [adder's] den" (11: 6-8). All of this marvelous prophecy concerns this coming Redeemer.

The fifty-third chapter you know well. "He was wounded for our transgressions, he was bruised for our iniquities: the chastisement of our peace was upon him;

and with his stripes we are healed" (v. 5).

As we look at these and the other prophecies, we see two pictures. We see a suffering Christ and we see a reigning Christ. We see Christ dying on a cross, wounded for our transgressions. We also see him sitting on a throne — on the throne of his father David. We are perplexed. There must be something wrong! How can Christ be both a suffering Christ and the reigning Christ, at the same time?

I think we can illustrate by a mountain range. One can look across to the highest range in the distance, but also at hills nearby. If you are familiar with the area, you may know that there is a valley in between. Stand near Knoxville, Tennessee, and look south toward the Smokies and you see what looks like one high range of mountains, but when you drive down by Maryville and turn east toward Gatlinburg, you find that you are entering into a valley with the mountains on both sides of you. The valley cannot be seen from Knoxville, yet it is there.

The prophet Isaiah looked and saw both the cross and the throne, but he didn't realize that in between that cross and the throne was the valley which we know as the *church age*. He saw the Christ, whose coming was to die for sin, as a suffering Messiah, but he also saw that the Messiah was to reign, was to be a ruler on a throne. The prophet probably couldn't quite understand because God had not revealed it fully. That is why that in our text that was read in the beginning, Peter said that the prophets tried to find the answer of this mystery of the suffering of Christ and the glory which is to follow. The prophets didn't see this great church age in which you and I live. They saw Christ in his first coming. They saw Christ in his second coming. But they didn't understand the period between.

There were hundreds of prophecies in this Bible about the first coming of Christ and every single one of them was fulfilled perfectly. Somebody said that there were thirty-three distinct prophecies in the Old Testament that were fulfilled in the events relating to the death and resurrection of Christ. Someone else said that there were 333 prophecies concerning the first coming of Christ, every one of which was perfectly fulfilled. W. A. Criswell names nineteen of those prophecies fulfilled in the first coming of Christ in *Why I Preach That the Bible Is Literally True*. He says this is a proof that the Bible is the Word of God because they were so perfectly fulfilled.

Part Yet to Be Fulfilled

There are, however, prophecies of events that have not yet happened. Christ is not yet on the throne of David, and the Bible said that he was going to be there. That word was given to Mary that he is to sit on the throne of David. Yet he is not. The world is not in a millennium. Men have not yet beaten their swords into plowshares. The animal kingdom has not found peace together. The picture in Isaiah that the lion and the lamb would lie down together, hasn't happened yet. The child putting his hand on the den of the cockatrice or the asp, hasn't happened.

Is it going to happen? We know that it is going to happen, first of all because no prophecy has failed, and second, because nothing is more clearly taught in the Bible, not only in the Old Testament, but also in the New Testament, than that Jesus is coming again. Jesus made clear that he was to die, but he also said, "I'll come back." He said, "I go to prepare a place for you and if I go and prepare a place, I will come again." A few commentators say that that means death. What are they thinking about? Christ doesn't come at the time of death. That isn't the second coming. This is not what he was talking about when he said that he would come again.

"For the Son of man shall come in the glory of his Father with his angels; and then he shall reward every man according to his works" (Matt. 16:27).

In Matthew 24 the disciples said, "Lord, what will be the sign of thy coming and of the end of the age?" He did not rebuke them, nor did he say, "You shouldn't ask for signs." He gave them signs. We shall see those signs in another message in this series.

Our Lord said in Matthew 24:30, "And then shall appear the sign of the Son of man in heaven: and then shall all the tribes of the earth mourn, and they shall see the Son of man coming in the clouds of heaven with power and great glory." Does that sound like death?

We turn to Luke 21:27-29: "And then shall they see the Son of man coming in a cloud with power and great glory. And when these things begin to come to pass, then look up, and lift up your heads; for your redemption draweth nigh."

Jesus said repeatedly that he is coming again. When he was taken up from the Mount of Olives, that beautiful mountain east of Jerusalem, we are told in the Acts 1:11 that the disciples watched as he was taken up, and two men in white apparel stood by them and said, "Ye men of Galilee, why stand ye gazing up into heaven? this same Jesus, which is taken up from you into heaven, shall so come [again] in like manner as ye have seen him go into heaven." He's coming back! Every New Testament writer says it. He's coming back! Indeed the New Testament closes with the words "Even so, come quickly, Lord Jesus!"

The hope of the world? It is in Jesus Christ. It is in the fact that he came the first time as God's provision of a

Redeemer to die for our sins. It is in the truth that he is
coming again in power and glory. He conquered death, he
went back to glory, and he is coming again! This is the
world's greatest coming event! Here is the world's hope
— the coming of Jesus Christ; the coming of the Eternal
King.

Billy Graham tells that he was a guest in the home of
an editor of the *New York Times*. After the meal, they
were sitting around in the living room talking and got to
discussing world conditions, and the situation seemed so
discouraging and dark, that a spirit of despair settled
over the group.

Then Billy said, "Wait a minute. You men are all looking at the wrong side. It is not hopeless. There is hope!"
Then he began to tell them about what the Bible says
concerning the coming of the Lord Jesus Christ, the
hope that is in him! He said one man who was listening
seemed fascinated, and when Dr. Graham had finished
describing the events of the return of Jesus, and their
meaning as the hope of the world, this man said, "That's
the most fantastic thing that I've ever heard in my life.
I've never heard that before. I've gone to church all my
life, but I've never heard that." Then he added, "This
is the first note of hope that I've heard in many years."

Yes, it is the world's one hope! If you look at what science says, if you look at what historians say, if you look
at what the military men say, you find all to be hopeless;
but when you look at your Bible then you know that there
is hope. That hope is Jesus Christ. Christians do not need
to be afraid. If one does not have Christ, he has no
hope. Yet, he can have hope because Christ died for all.
The prayer of Christians is that all men will allow Jesus
Christ to be their hope.

3

In The Twinkling of An Eye

1 Corinthians 15:52

In the preceding chapters we have learned that the Bible is a book of prophecy, and that prophecy centers about a Man, the Lord Jesus Christ. We discovered that the prophets presented a twofold picture of Christ, first as a suffering Savior, and then as a king in his glory. We also found that his coming as a king is related to what the Bible calls the second coming, and that great sections of the prophetic word relate to that event. We found that every prophecy concerning Christ's first coming as a savior was literally fulfilled. This gives us strong reason for believing that prophecies concerning the second coming will be fulfilled in the same way. There are hundreds of verses in the Old Testament which evidently refer to our Lord's second coming, and more than 300 New Testament verses speak of it.

As we seek to understand the Bible's picture of the second coming of Christ, we discover that there are at least three major schools of theological interpretation of it.

The word "millennial" means "thousand," and comes from the references in Revelation 20 concerning a thousand-year period related to the Lord's return. In theological interpretation it refers to a thousand-year reign of Christ on the earth. There is disagreement as to whether this is an exact figure or an approximate one. There is a position called postmillennialism.

The *postmillennial* position is based upon the belief that Christianity will convert the world and then Christ's king-

dom will come in. Adherents believe that the preaching
of the gospel will be so effective and the work of the
churches so successful, that the world will come into a
golden age of peace and prosperity.

As one writer stated, the whole world will come into
the "train of Christ." Many people who hold this interpretation believed that the twentieth century would be
the beginning of the millennium. However, conditions
have been such in this century that many now question
whether the world will even last through this century.
The situation is now so bad, that postmillennialism is
virtually an abandoned theological viewpoint.

A second interpretation is called *amillennialism*. The
amillennialists do believe in the second coming of Christ,
but reject the idea of a millennial reign of Christ on earth.
They believe that the second coming will bring the judgment, the consummation of things on earth, and the
introduction of eternity. This is a simplified statement of
the position, but at least gives a general view of it. The
amillennialists reject the idea that Israel as a nation has a
future. They do not believe that prophecies concerning
the Jew, the "tribulation," or the prophecies of Revelation
are in any sense to be taken literally. They say that most
of the prophecies both of the Old and the New Testaments
that have reference to a kingdom, to the Jew, or to events
related to the Lord's return, are not to be taken literally
but *spiritually*.

The third position is the *premillennial* interpretation.
The premillennialist believes that Christ *literally* is returning to the earth and that the Bible reveals numerous
events which are related to his coming. They believe that
he will set up a kingdom, and actually will reign for a
thousand years, sitting upon what the Bible calls "the
throne of David." They believe that God is not through
with the Jews as a nation, and that numerous prophecies

concerning their future are yet to be fulfilled. Even pre-millennialists are not fully agreed upon the details of the second coming, but they are together in their thinking on the major details of the return.

After thirty years of careful study of Bible prophecy, I am by conviction a premillennialist, and the things which follow in this book are based upon that interpretation. I do want it understood, however, that I have no desire to appear dogmatic, for I may be mistaken.

Sometimes I have said to friends who take a different view, "When the Lord comes, and we stand before him, I am sure that he will show us which one was mistaken." I am glad that this is not a point of fellowship among most Christians. Both the premillennialist and the amillennialist agree that Christ is coming, and that it is important for every person to so live as to be ready for that coming. The details are not so important that we spend all of our time on them. The great truth is the event itself. Nevertheless, I believe that when the Bible gives revelation concerning events pertaining to the Lord's advent, we should diligently try to understand them.

We must add that there is a fourth position which some seem to espouse, which is spoken of jokingly as *promillennialism.* Those holding this position simply say, "I am for it. I do not know much about it, but I am for it." I heard one outstanding preacher say, "I am not on the time and place committee, but on the reception committee. I want to be there to welcome the Lord when he comes."

Christians are divided on the interpretations of the event, but those who believe the Bible do look for the Lord to return. I cannot agree with those who say that it is impossible to understand prophecy, therefore there is no use wasting time trying to study it. With all my heart I believe that we need to study everything in the Bible, and that includes prophecy. When we do give serious study to it, we find that its meaning begins to unfold, and we find a glorious revelation within the Bible's pages. It gives meaning to history and to life itself. Moreover, understanding and believing great prophetic truth will make us better Christians, and create a desire for more dedicated Christian living.

Thus we approach the great Bible truths which we shall study in this and following chapters. We believe that they are important. We believe that they can be understood when carefully studied. We believe that they are to be taken literally, unless it is clear that they are figurative. We believe that they are given to help Christians understand what God is doing, and what he has planned for the future.

In this chapter we shall consider the very first things which are going to happen to Christians when Jesus comes — in the very first event of his return. In the next chapter we shall see what this coming will mean to the world, and in the following chapter, what will happen, after the main events of the return are completed. We believe that God has revealed many of the details of these things in his Word, and shall try to understand them now.

Again, we remind you that we cannot be dogmatic in what we say concerning these matters, since we may be misinterpreting or misunderstanding them. Here are the events as the Bible seems to be presenting them. Our purpose is to try to understand what is going to happen to Christians when the Lord returns.

An Imaginary Chart

I do not have a chart, nor do I plan to use one, but it will be helpful to you in understanding the relationship of these events if you have, at least in your mind's eye, a chart-like outline of what we are saying. To help us with this mental picture, imagine that you are sitting in an auditorium with the choir loft centered behind the pulpit as it is in most churches. Let us allow the choir area to be the center of the chart. On your left, as you face it, there is a vertical post, and on the right is another vertical post, and of course, there is the line of the arch reaching from post to post which encloses the choir area.

Now let us consider that the post on your left represents the first event of the Lord's return, which is called the *rapture*. Out beyond that post is a wall and we can imagine it as reaching on and on, for that represents the age in which we are living, the *church age*. It began at Christ's first coming, for he established his church while he was here on the earth. It will be concluded at the moment the trumpet of the Lord sounds and the events of our Lord's return begin. So we are living in the day beyond the left vertical post. Already it has lasted almost 2,000 years, and we do not know how much longer it will last, for we do not know when the Lord will return.

However, one of these days this church age is going to end suddenly, in what is theologically called the rapture. The second coming actually is in two phases, the *rapture* when the Lord comes in the air for his saints, and the *revelation* when the Lord comes down to the earth with his saints.

Let us allow the post on the left of the choir (your left as you face it) to represent the first phase of his coming, the rapture, and the vertical post on your right to represent the second phase, the revelation. In between is the period represented by the choir loft itself, which we shall call the *tribulation*. This will be our next study.

Beyond the revelation, the post to your right, is the period after the Lord's return and the Bible reveals many things which are to happen then. That will be the third message in this series on what is coming.

Now we are thinking of the very first event of the

Lord's return, the rapture. In this study we shall deal
with the things which will happen to you, if you are a
Christian, when the Lord returns. Actually, whatever
may be one's theological interpretation of the return of the
Lord — premillennial, amillennial, or promillennial, or
even postmillennial — this is the most important phase of
all of the events of the Lord's coming. However we may
disagree concerning other matters, we do believe that he
is coming, and do want to know what will happen when
he comes. As we already have said, this interpretation is
from the premillennial view.

The Rapture

What is to happen first? The rapture. This is when the
Lord comes for his saints. Let us read the Scripture because that is our only source of knowledge of this.

How shall we interpret Scripture? David L. Cooper
said, "When the plain sense of the Scripture makes common sense and no other sense, then take every word of
its primary ordinary usual literal meaning, unless the facts
of the immediate context, studied in the light of related
passages and axiomatic and fundamental truths in the
Word, indicate clearly otherwise." He says, allow the Bible to say what it says and accept it, unless it is clear that
it means something else.

In the light of this let us look at some passages. First,
let us consider 1 Corinthians 15:51. You have read this
or heard it read again and again in connection with
funerals, but actually it is not a reference to a funeral.
Look at Paul's words. He has been discussing the gospel
in the opening part of this chapter, then he considers the
resurrection of Christ, and then he speaks about the
changes that are to happen to our bodies when we die and
are raised again. But look at verse 51.

"Behold, I shew you a mystery; we shall not all sleep,

but we shall all be changed." Not every Christian is going to sleep in the sleep of death. He calls death a sleep. We "shall not all die," he says. Some people as Christians are not going to have to die. If we are here when Jesus comes again, we shall go without dying. That is what Paul says.

Listen to his words: "I shew you a mystery." Here is a mysterious revelation from God. "We shall not all sleep, but we shall all be changed." He is talking to Christians. "In a moment, in the twinkling of an eye, at the last trump: for the trumpet shall sound, and the dead shall be raised incorruptible, and we shall be changed. For this corruptible must put on incorruption, and this mortal must put on immortality. So when this corruptible shall have put on incorruption, and this mortal shall have put on immortality, then shall be brought to pass the saying that is written, Death is swallowed up in victory" (vv. 52-54).

What has he said? In a moment, in the twinkling of an eye, when the trumpet sounds, two things are going to happen. The dead in Christ are going to be raised and the living Christians of that day are going to be changed. Can we be sure that is what it means? Turn to 1 Thessalonians 4:13.

"But I would not have you to be ignorant, brethren, concerning them which are asleep." Now these people were concerned about those who had died. They wondered what was going to happen to them. That apparently was what occasioned the writing of these words. "I would not have you to be ignorant, brethren, concerning them which are asleep, that ye sorrow not, even as others which have no hope."

He is saying that Christians do not need to be disturbed and worried about those who have died in Christ. They have a hope that the unsaved do not have, so they do not have to worry about death.

"For if we believe that Jesus died and rose again, even so them also which sleep in Jesus will God bring with him" (v. 14). The bodies are in the cemetery. The spirits have gone on to be with the Lord.

My father was a Baptist preacher. He died when I was seven years of age. I am sure that he went to be with the Lord. Not long ago I stood by his grave in the little cemetery in a country churchyard in Illinois. I'm sure that his body went back to dust a long time ago. I stood by that grave marker but I was not depressed, for I knew that his spirit went on to be with the Lord at the time of his death.

In 1955 my son, a twenty-year-young preacher, died. We laid his body in a Memorial Park, by the Shores of the Gulf of Mexico, between Gulfport and Biloxi in Mississippi. One of these days if the Lord doesn't come first, my body will be laid there, too. My spirit, too, will go to be with the Lord. Paul said, "absent from the body, present with the Lord." And Paul says here that the spirits of these who are asleep — "them also which are asleep in Jesus" — will God bring with him.

Bring with him? What does that mean? Well, he tells in the next verses. "For this we say unto you by the word of the Lord, that we which are alive, and remain unto the coming of the Lord, shall not [precede] them that are asleep. [The King James Version says "prevent" but the Greek word means "precede." We are not going to hold them back. They shall rise, and we shall be changed.] For the Lord himself shall descend from heaven with a shout, with the voice of the archangel, and with the trump of God; and the dead in Christ shall rise first" (vv. 15-16). This is the very first event of the second coming.

Think of the day when graves in the cemeteries of the world burst open.

A young man said to me, "You know, when a person dies and the body goes back to dust, it may be scattered. It can be scattered and it can become part of another body. What about that?" I said, "I think my God is great enough to gather all the atoms of man that he wants put together to form a new body. I'm not worried about God being able to do that."

Listen to it. "The dead in Christ shall rise first." Then we who are alive and remain shall be caught up together with them in the clouds. The dead in Christ are caught up and Christians who are still on the earth at that moment will, in a twinkling, be caught up to be with the Lord in the air. That's what it says. Now if it doesn't mean that, what does it mean? Let me repeat it: "The trumpet of the Lord shall sound, the dead in Christ shall rise, then we who are alive and remain shall be caught up together with them in the clouds, to meet the Lord in the air: and so shall we ever be with the Lord."

The trumpet will sound. Trumpets were used by the Jews in many ways in their worship. The trumpet would sound when the people were called together for worship. The trumpet was sounded for their peace days, and the trumpet was sounded when their men marched off to war. The trumpets were sounded when Solomon opened the temple, and on all the great occasions, the trumpet sounded. In the book of Revelation we are told about the trumpets sounding, announcing the judgments of God on the earth in the tribulation period which shall be considered in the next chapter.

The greatest sound of the trumpet will be when the trumpet of the Lord sounds around the earth and the saved will be caught up to meet the Lord in the air and the dead in Christ raised up. That is the rapture. The

Bible says that it will be "in the twinkling of an eye." Can you measure the twinkle of your eye? It will be that quickly. The trumpet sounds, and suddenly the saved are gone. What a marvelous message we have here. You can't measure a twinkle, but that shows how suddenly it's going to be. And notice what is to happen.

There will be a taking. The trumpet will sound. All the graves of all the saved, all the saved dead who are out in the seas or out in the desert — all of them will be raised up with new bodies. Those of us who are Christians suddenly will be caught up to be with the Lord. In Matthew 24:40 Jesus said, "Two shall be in the field; the one shall be taken, and the other left." Here are two farmers working in the wheat harvest, or in the corn, or in the fields with some other crop, and suddenly one of them is gone. That is what Christ says. Two men will be in the field. "Two women shall be grinding at the mill." Here are two women working, one of them saved, the other unsaved, and suddenly the saved person is gone. One shall be taken and the other left. And in the next verse he says, "Watch therefore: for ye know not what hour your Lord doth come."

In the book of Mark we have the same truth, while in Luke 17:34-37 we have the same truth in a different form. "I tell you, in that night there shall be two men in one bed; the one shall be taken, and the other shall be left. Two women shall be grinding together; the one shall be taken, and the other left. Two men shall be in the field; the one shall be taken, and the other left."

What does it mean? Surely it means just what it says. Suppose that while I am standing preaching, the Lord Jesus were to come. That would be this first phase of his coming — his rapture. The Lord would come in the air for his saints and the trumpet would begin to sound like the thunders of the heaven and suddenly every saved

person in the congregation would be gone. Everyone —
in the twinkling of an eye. No wonder Paul said it's a
mystery. You say, "Brother Odle, that's fantastic!" Yes,
it is fantastic, but it's what the Scripture says. And either
you accept what the Scripture says or simply throw it
away; because if it doesn't mean what it says, then we
do not know what it means.

Now just think what is going to happen in the world
at that moment of the rapture. A Christian man may be
flying a big airliner and suddenly he is gone and that airliner is without a pilot. Suppose the pilot and the as-
sistant pilot both are Christians — suddenly they are
gone. A high-speed train may be rushing down the track
with a Christian engineer, and suddenly he is gone. On
the highways, the interstates, cars will be whizzing along
and suddenly many of them will go out of control because the drivers are gone.

You say "Brother Odle, you're out of your head."
No, I'm not! I'm saying what Jesus said. He said, "Two
shall be in a bed — one taken and the other left. Two
shall be in a field — one taken and the other left."
When Jesus comes, the rapture will occur. It is a wonderful thing to think about if you're ready, if you have Jesus
Christ as your Savior. If you have been born again
through faith in the Lord Jesus and your name is written
in glory, then you can say, "Lord, I'm ready." Because in
that moment every grave of saved people will be opened,
and all of us as Christians will be caught up to be with
the Lord in the air. The Bible says, "We ever will be with
the Lord." This is the first thing that is to happen. This
is the next event in prophetic history as revealed in the
Bible.

The rapture will be *imminent*. That word means that it
may happen at any moment. It may be delayed another
thousand years, but it could happen before you finish

reading this sentence. Jesus said in Matthew 24:44, "Therefore be ye also ready: for in such an hour as ye think not the Son of man cometh."

This is the very first event of the second coming of Christ, and reveals why it is so important that men be saved. Christ came the first time to die and provide a way of salvation. He is coming the second time to receive those who are saved unto himself. For the saved it will be a glorious day, but for the unsaved, a terrible one. How tragic to be left behind when the Lord comes; to be left in a world without a Christian. This will happen to many on that day when the trumpet suddenly begins to sound and the Lord's return is announced.

Transformation

Millions of people will suddenly be taken up in that moment when the Lord comes . . . both the dead Christians of the ages past, and the living Christians of that hour. What will happen to them when they suddenly are caught up to meet their Lord? First Corinthians 15:52-53 says, "We shall be changed. For this corruptible must put on incorruption, and this mortal must put on immortality." In that moment when we are caught up to be with the Lord, these old bodies which now are subject to disease and death, will be changed. Suffering and pain will be no more. These experiences come to us here because our bodies are mortal, but in that moment a new, glorious body will be provided.

John speaks a wonderful word concerning this. "Beloved, now are we the sons of God, and it doth not yet appear what we shall be: but we know that, when he shall appear, we shall be like him; for we shall see him as he is" (1 John 3:2). The dead in Christ will be changed, and the living will be changed. All will have new, immortal bodies, glorified bodies like unto that of Christ.

This is the transformation which is to take place in that glad moment.

Judgment of Christians

The Scriptures seem to teach that this is that hour when Christians stand before the judgment seat of Christ. According to the Bible judgment is something which every person must face. However, I do not believe in a general judgment.

It appears that those who stand before the great white throne judgment in Revelation 20 are unsaved people. However, Paul says clearly in 2 Corinthians 5:10, "For we must all appear before the judgment seat of Christ; that everyone may receive the things done in his body, according to that he hath done, whether it be good or bad." Paul was writing to Christians, so he must be talking about their judgment.

Every one of us, even as Christians, must give an account of the lives we have lived, and of the things which we have done. Judgment is not to determine whether one is going to heaven or hell. Did you think it was? No! That is determined here on this earth. The decision of whether you are going to hell or heaven is made on the basis of what you do with Jesus Christ. If you accept him as Savior, the judgment of your sins is laid on him, and the future judgments are not to determine whether you go to heaven or to hell, but to the Christian it is to determine what rewards God is to give you. It is to judge your life as a Christian.

To understand this let us turn to 1 Corinthians 3:10. "Let every man take heed how he buildeth thereupon." He is talking about the foundation.

The following verses say, "For other foundation can no man lay than that is laid, which is Jesus Christ. Now if any man build upon this foundation gold, silver, precious stones, wood, hay, stubble;

"Every man's work shall be made manifest: for the day shall declare it, because it shall be revealed by fire: and the fire shall try every man's work of what sort it is." This is not talking about hell fire. This is talking about judgment. "If any man's work shall be burned, he shall suffer loss: but he himself shall be saved, yet so as by fire."

He says your life is going to be judged and my life is going to be judged after we are caught up with the Lord in the air. The Lord Jesus is going to call me before him because the Bible says he is the judge. He will say, "Joe Odle, here is your record. We have the record in the book. Why didn't you serve me better? Why didn't you pray more? Why weren't you a better witness? You had so many opportunities to witness. There are so many things you could have done." I will stand there before him ashamed of the things wherein I have failed.

Perhaps in some things he will say, "Joe, you did well in this. Well done thou good and faithful servant." Everyone of us is going to stand there. What kind of a Christian have you been? What kind of a church member have you been? What has your prayer life been? What about this matter of your attitude toward your neighbors and friends? How have you treated your family? Have there been things that you have hidden behind in the darkness?

In that day all the skeletons are going to come out of the closets. Thank God we are not going to have to go to hell for them, because these sins are not charged to us as far as our going to hell is concerned. Romans 4:8 says, "Blessed is the man to whom the Lord will not impute sin." The word "impute" means charge and the reference is to the Christian. Sin is not charged to me as far as my having to go to hell for it. If it were, then everyone of us would go to hell because Christ's death was not sufficient.

Thank God, my sins are charged to him. I am a child of God. As his child he has to whip me. "Whom the Lord loveth he chasteneth." But he whips me and keeps me. *Not one child of God ever will be lost.* When I stand before him, there will be rewards. Maybe he will say, "Joe, I had these rewards. I had so many things I wanted to give you, but you failed to obey me, and to do what I wanted you to do." Could my works be "burned"? Did I build on "wood, hay, stubble," the materials which are consumed when you place them on the fire? Will I have empty hands when I stand before the Lord, because all of the works to which I gave my life were not the eternal things? Is my Christian life such that it is building with "gold, silver, precious stone"?

The Bible has much to say about crowns and rewards. Every man is rewarded according to his works. This is not talking about salvation, for that is not a reward, but a free gift. Rewards are for service. That is why we urge Christians to be godly in living, faithful in their stewardship, and diligent in service. That is why we urge Christian witnessing and support of the church and of the whole kingdom program of our Lord. As Christians use their time and talents for the Lord, they are "laying up treasures in heaven" and are getting ready for that day when they shall "give account" to the Lord. How wonderful it will be in that hour, if he can say to us, "Well done!"

People have said to me, "I'll be satisfied just to get into heaven." The truth of the matter is that they will not be. Certainly, it will be glorious to be with him and to receive the eternal things he has prepared for us, but what are we going to say when he asks us why we did not serve him more faithfully?

What will be our feeling when he asks why we became so busy with the world that we did not have time to witness

of him? This should make us want to do our best. The
judgment is certain, and every one of us must face him.
This is why your pastor stands up and preaches to you
about Christian living and pleads with you to do God's
will. The Bible says in Hebrews that he is the "shepherd,"
responsible for your souls. My heart breaks when I think
about people who may have gone to hell because I didn't
work hard enough or I didn't pray hard enough, or I didn't
visit enough, or I didn't go and urge them enough. They
just slipped out into eternity and when I stand before the
Lord, he may say, "Joe, if you had just gone one more
time, or had just worked a little harder. . . ." Judgment
is going to come when we meet the Lord in the air.

The Marriage of the Lamb

Now there is something else that the Bible says is going
to happen then and it seems that it happens just at this
time. The Bible talks about a marriage of the Lamb. In
Revelation 19:7-10 we read:

**Let us be glad and rejoice, and give honour to
him: for the marriage of the Lamb is come, and his
wife hath made herself ready. And to her was
granted that she should be arrayed in fine linen,
clean and white: for the fine linen is the righteousness of saints. And he saith unto me, Write, blessed
are they which are called unto the marriage supper
of the Lamb. And he saith unto me, These are the
true sayings of God. And I fell at his feet to worship him. And he said unto me, See thou do it not;
I am thy fellow-servant, and of thy brethren that have
the testimony of Jesus: worship God.**

John was thrilled by this picture of the saved of the ages
becoming the bride of the Lord Jesus. Paul evidently was
thinking about this in Ephesians 5.

"Husbands, love your wives, even as Christ also loved the church, and gave himself for it; That he might sanctify and cleanse it with the washing of water by the word, That he might present it to himself a glorious church, not having spot, or wrinkle, or any such thing; but that it should be holy and without blemish" (vv. 25-27).

Apparently, even here, Paul is thinking of that day when we stand as the bride of the Lord Jesus Christ. I think this is to come after the rapture. First we are caught up, then we are judged, and then comes that glorious moment when we are presented to the Lord. Paul talks about it here, "a bride adorned for her husband," glorious, "without spot or wrinkle."

I'm sure you have attended beautiful weddings. The preacher stands in front of the pulpit. In comes the young man, the groom, and the best man and they stand beside the preacher, and then come all the attendants down the aisle and take their places. Still, everyone is eagerly watching. They are waiting for that moment when the organ sounds out "Here Comes the Bride." Through the door comes the bride. She is beautifully attired, spotless, glorious, adorned for her husband. The groom beholds her with eyes of love.

Paul uses this figure to picture the Lord's relationship to his church. He says that Christ loves the church, and that he wants to present it unto himself, "a glorious church, not having spot or wrinkle." Surely this must be the time when that presentation will take place. The Bible does not tell us much about the marriage of the Lamb, but it does tell us that it is going to happen. If I understand what the Bible is saying, you are going to be in it if you are a child of God.

Revelation

The second phase of the Lord's return, as I understand

it, is called the revelation. This is the moment when the Lord comes on down to the earth with his saints. In the rapture, which we have seen earlier in this chapter, the saints are caught up to meet the Lord in the air. Now, with his saints, he comes down to the earth. We shall study more about it in the next chapter, but let us look at it closely enough here to know what it means.

In the book of Jude, verse 14 we read: "And Enoch also, the seventh from Adam, prophesied of these, saying, Behold, the Lord cometh with ten thousands of his saints."

Other passages speak of every eye seeing him, and of his standing on the Mount of Olives. Still other passages help us see the complete picture. This is the revelation, the second phase of the second coming. It appears to come at the close of the tribulation period, and probably about seven years after the rapture. Later we will show why we say that.

With his saints the Lord now comes to the earth, this time as the conqueror. He will be in power and great glory, and the Bible says that we shall live and reign with him a thousand years on the earth. Who is going to do that? The saved.

Are you saved? If Jesus were to come today, if the trumpet were to sound, would you be left behind or would you go out to meet the Lord in the air? If you are saved, if you have been born again, if you are a child of God, then when this trumpet sounds and the saved are taken out, you will go with them in that great moment of meeting the Lord Jesus Christ. But if you are not saved, then you will be left behind. These glorious things we have seen are not for you. Instead, you can look to dreadful things described in the next chapter, or to things beyond death as seen in the following one.

4

The World's Most Terrible "Week"

Daniel 9:24-27

This, the fourth message of this series, is the most difficult to present because it is so involved. It is the most difficult to understand because there are so many facets to it, and yet it is so important that I think we cannot fail to look at it and try to understand it. The Bible says that we should "study to show ourselves approved unto God, . . . rightly dividing the word of truth." When I hear a man say, "I just can't understand Revelation, or any Bible prophecy, so I'm not going to bother with it," I am convinced that he is wrong. The Bible is given to us for us study, and we ought to try to understand what God is saying to us, even in the most difficult passages.

We are discussing the world's most terrible "week" and I put the word "week" in quotation marks because it is not an ordinary week, but a "week" of years. It is Daniel's seventieth week.

Please do not be disturbed if you do not fully understand all that we find in this chapter, for if you are a child of God, you are not going to be here in this week anyway. In the preceding chapter we saw that the saved of this age will be taken up when the trumpet of the Lord sounds and the Lord comes in the air, and the saved on earth who are living at that time and the dead in Christ are going to rise and meet the Lord in the air. The Tribulation Period or Daniel's seventieth week immediately will follow on the earth, so those who are saved now will not be here. The

61

world is going to be left without a Christian. I think it
is seven years and later you will see why I think that. It
may be more, but it seems that it is a seven-year period.
It is the period of years while the Christians are in the
air with the Lord. Let us consider prophecies of what will
happen in this period as if each event were a part of a
jigsaw puzzle. We shall look at the different parts and
then we shall try to put them together. There are a number of events which the Bible seems to say will happen
in this period.

The Seventieth Week

First we must examine the prophecy of a "week" which
is coming. We turn to the book of Daniel, chapter 9,
one of the most wonderful chapters in the Bible. It is the
chapter where Daniel the prophet is in prayer for his people and in answer to that prayer God sends a messenger
(v. 23) to tell Daniel that he is beloved in heaven, that
God has heard his prayer, and that he is giving him a
special revelation. Verse 24 begins one of the great prophetic pictures of the Bible. It is one that confuses people
unless they really rightly divide the Word of truth. Let
us examine it carefully.

"Seventy weeks are determined upon thy people." The
word "weeks" there is the Hebrew word *shabu'im* which
simply is "sevens" and the translation is made weeks,
"seventy weeks are determined upon they people." Daniel
had been praying for his people, the Jews, and so "thy people" must refer to the Jews. We have to keep this in mind.
This is a prophecy that relates to the Jews. Indeed, all the
prophecies we are going to study in this chapter relate to
the Jews. Somebody has asked, "Is the United States in
this prophecy?" If it is, it is hidden. What I mean is that
there is nothing that identifies the United States, but if

the United States is not there it is because there are prophecies concerning nations and how they are related to Jews.

The passage says, "thy people and thy holy city." What is the Holy City? Jerusalem. God says to him, these prophesied 70 weeks are determined upon thy people — the Jewish people — and upon thy holy city. Now he gives five or six things that are to be accomplished in this period. "To finish the transgression." To bring to an end the sinfulness, the sinning of this people as a nation. To finish it and to make an end of it and to "make reconciliation for iniquity."

There is to be a provision of a way of salvation and of a way to bring in everlasting righteousness. Men have dreamed of everlasting righteousness and have talked about everlasting righteousness, and God says here to the prophet, Daniel, that there is a seventy-week period that is going to bring these things in to seal up the vision and prophecy. All the prophecies and visions concerning Israel are to be finished. They are to be completed. "To anoint the most Holy." This is the anointing of the Messiah, the most holy One.

Now, look at the next verse, "Know therefore and understand, that from the going forth of the commandment to restore and to build Jerusalem unto the Messiah the Prince shall be seven weeks, and threescore and two weeks."

Here is a definite date and if Jewish leaders had simply studied Daniel's prophecy carefully, they would have known when the Messiah would come. He says that there will be seven weeks and threescore and two weeks from a certain date. He says that the street shall be built again, and the wall, "even in troublous times."

A careful study of Bible history reveals that there were

four commands related to rebuilding at Jerusalem. Three
of them are in the book of Ezra, but as you examine them
you find that everyone of them relates to the building of the
Temple. They do not relate to the rebuilding of the city
of Jerusalem itself. There is only one command given by
an outside king to go back to Jerusalem and to rebuild
the city and to rebuild the walls. That is found in the
book of Nehemiah. And Nehemiah tells us the date. He
gives the twentieth year of Artaxerxes that this command
was given to go back and rebuild the city of Jerusalem, and
historians have found that this was the year 445 B.C.

Now Daniel is told that from the day that this command is given until the coming of the Messiah shall be
seven weeks and three score and two weeks — seven weeks
and sixty-two weeks and as has been said, as we study it
we recognize that he is talking about weeks of years. The
Jews understood this because the Old Testament speaks
often about weeks of years. So it should have been understood.

The first section here was the time of the rebuilding.
It took about forty-nine years for the rebuilding and it was
rebuilt in troublous times, but the Messiah didn't come
right then. He was to come sixty-two weeks later. Sixty-
two and seven are sixty-nine. Now what are sixty-nine
weeks of years? Quickly we see it is 483 years. These
were 483 Jewish years. The Jewish year was not the same
length as ours; it was 360 days. That is what the Jews
counted and 483 Jewish years from the day that the command was given by the king for Nehemiah to go back and
build the wall, brings us to the time of Jesus' ministry.

Indeed Sir Robert Anderson, a great English Bible
scholar, says in his book *The Coming King* that it actually
brings us to the very day of Christ's triumphal entry. Now
if Sir Robert Anderson is right, and he has given a lifetime

to study it, then the 483 years ended the very day when the people sang Hosanna to the King. As the prophecy revealed, 483 years from the command to rebuild the city, the Messiah came. But the Jews rejected him. They refused him! And they asked the Romans to nail him to a cross. Now note the next words.

"And after threescore and two weeks [that's after this 483 years] shall Messiah be cut off, but not for himself." The note in the margin says it means "shall have nothing!" (KJV). As far as the Jewish people were concerned they rejected him, they cut him off, and he was nothing. When did it happen? After this 483 years had passed as revealed to Daniel.

Now that is 69 weeks, but in Daniel 9:24 he says "seventy weeks," so there is one week still missing. Yet the prophecy continues. Look at verse 26: "And the people of the prince that shall come shall destroy the city and the sanctuary."

Now we know who destroyed the city and the sanctuary. It was Rome, for Titus came with his Roman armies, and in the year A.D. 70 completely destroyed the city of Jerusalem. He is said to have killed a million Jews, and to have taken into captivity hundreds of thousands of others who were scattered to the ends of the earth. Now these were "the people" of somebody else who is in this picture — "the people of the prince that shall come shall destroy the city and the sanctuary; and the end thereof shall be with a flood, and unto the end of the war desolations are determined." That is, there is to be a flood of desolation and war in connection with this destruction. Historically the prophecy relates to the Jew, and for them it will be like a flood of desolation.

It seems evident that God quit counting time with the Jews at the moment of their rejection of Christ and Christ's

crucifixion. As far as counting time with them as a nation,
it ended right then. An interval came. In that interval is
the church age in which you and I live. God is not counting time with the Jews for the time being, but evidently
his counting will begin again when the church age ends
and we as Christians have been taken up. Then this seventieth week will come. Space does not allow us to explore
this further, but that is what many prophetic students
see.

Many believe that Daniel's seventieth week is this period
on the earth after the saved have been taken out in the
rapture and before they come back with him in the
revelation. This is Daniel's seventieth week and it is to be
a most terrible week. The Bible speaks of "the day of
Jacob's trouble." This is one of the designations of it in
Jeremiah. Jesus speaks of it in Matthew 24 as a day of
great tribulation. Many Bible scholars believe this is
Daniel's seventieth week.

Let us return to the Daniel reference. "And he shall
confirm the covenant with many for one week" (9:27).
Note the "he." Who is he? Evidently he is this "prince"
who is to come mentioned in verse 26. Not the Messiah,
but another prince who is to come and he shall confirm a
covenant with the Jewish people, for one week. Is this the
missing seventieth week? Now understand we're collecting
parts of a puzzle and we shall put them together before
we are finished, but let's simply examine them now.

"And in the midst of the week [in the middle of this
week, three and a half years] he shall cause the sacrifice
and the oblation to cease." This still is "the prince that
shall come" and he makes a covenant with the Jews for a
week, and they begin their offerings again. In the middle
of the week, he stops them.

This agreement that he has made with the Jews as a

nation allows them to start their sacrifices and offerings once more in their Temple, which makes us know that the Temple is to be rebuilt. The question often has been raised by many as to how the Jews can rebuild a Temple when a Muhammadan mosque is setting right where the old Temple used to be.

I read something interesting in an issue of a magazine that came to my desk. In this article written by a man who had just been to Jerusalem, it was stated that he had learned, when he was in Jerusalem, that the place where the offerings were made in the Temple actually was not where the mosque now stands but just west of it.

He said that the real heart of the Temple area where the sacrifices and offerings were made in both the Temple of Solomon, and also in that of Herod which was there in the days of Jesus, is on the same grounds but just west of where the present Mosque of Omar or the Muhammadan mosque now stands.

He suggested that the Jews could build the Temple and not have to disturb the mosque at all. Scholars long have wondered how the Temple could be rebuilt. The mosque is there and if you tear it down the Muhammadan world will quickly rise up. This writer said that there is a way that the Temple can be built without too serious conflict with Muslims. In whatever way it is done, the Jews are going to have a Temple. They are going to start their offerings again and in the midst of the week, this prince who is to come, is going to stop them. That is what this Scripture says. "He shall cause the sacrifice and the oblation to cease, and for the overspreading of abominations he shall make it desolate, even until the consummation, and that determined shall be poured upon the desolate." It's a strange word, but it seems to mean that there's going to be a terribly tragic time. Now that is our first picture.

Here is a week — Daniel's seventieth week that is yet to come to the earth.

Israel

Now let's consider a second part in this puzzle. For this second picture we must turn back to Ezekiel 37. This will be more seriously considered later but we must briefly consider it here.

This is one of the great chapters of prophecy because it tells of Israel again living as a nation and being back in her own land. In Ezekiel 34 to 36 we have passage after passage saying that the Jew is going to come back to the Holy Land. Chapter 36 says that the land will "become like a garden of Eden" (v. 35). Those of you who have been there know that this is happening now.

Chapter 37 is about a vision of Ezekiel. The prophet says that the Spirit set him in the midst of a valley which was full of dry bones, and he was asked the question in verse 3: "Can these bones live?" He answered, "Thou knowest." Then the Spirit said that he was going to cause them to come together again and "live."

The angel messenger told the prophet to speak and prophesy. "So I prophesied as I was commanded: and as I prophesied, there was a noise, and, behold a shaking, and the bones came together, bone to his bone" (v. 7). Our young people sometimes sing a spiritual which they have made into a popular song, "Dry Bones." They sing about one bone being added to another. It is based upon this passage. The bones come together. Now notice what was meant. In verses 11-14 we have the explanation.

"Then he said unto me, Son of man, these bones are the whole house of Israel: behold, they say, Our bones are dried, and our hope is lost: we are cut off for our parts. Therefore prophesy, and say unto them, Thus saith the

Lord God; Behold, O my people, I will open your graves, and cause you to come up out of your graves, and bring you into the land of Israel. And ye shall know that I am the Lord, when I have opened your graves, O my people, and brought you up out of your graves. And shall put my Spirit in you, and ye shall live, and I shall place you in your own land."

This is the second picture in our puzzle. The Jewish people are to be back in their own land when this seventieth week of Daniel, or the time of tribulation comes, because this is a week of years in which God will be dealing with the Jews and it will happen when they are back in their own land. In years gone by, many said, "That can never happen. Israel can never live again as a nation."

When Bible scholars 100 years and more ago said that Israel would again become a nation, they were sneered at and ridiculed. The attitude was that Israel was scattered to the ends of the earth, and her people could never be back in their own land again. Jerusalem never would belong to the Jews again.

Today, they are back in their own land, and they do have control of Jerusalem, and they have no intention ever of leaving again. In this "week" that is coming, the Jews must be back in their own land. That is the second picture in our puzzle. First of all, *there is a week that is coming*. Second, *the Jews are back in their own land*.

Tribulation

Now look at a third part of this puzzle. This is to be a period of tribulation. Turning back to Daniel, let us look at 12:1. "And at that time shall Michael stand up, the great prince which standeth for the children of thy people: and there shall be a time of trouble, such as never was since there was a nation even to that same time: and at

that time thy people shall be delivered [now *thy people*
again is the Jews], every one that shall be found written
in the book."

God is saying to Daniel, there's coming a day of trouble
to the Jewish people such as the world never has known.

Turn to Matthew 24:21 to see Christ's confirmation of
this. "For then shall be great tribulation, such as was not
since the beginning of the world to this time, no, nor
ever shall be."

The prophecy is of a time of trouble. Many scholars believe that the book of Revelation, chapters 6 to 19, is a
description of this day of trouble, the seventieth week of
Daniel. They see these chapters as a description of this
day of tribulation such as the world never has known.
These scholars believe that this section of the book of
Revelation is a prophecy concerning this week.

Beginning in Revelation 6 we see four horsemen described. The first is a white horse. Some scholars say this
is Christ, but I would answer no. Christ on a white horse
is in the nineteenth chapter. This white horseman evidently is the antichrist, that man we already have heard
about in Daniel and about whom we shall see more in the
next part of this chapter. This white horse leads the way
and is followed by other horses.

The second one is red and is to take peace from the
earth, and the third one is black and is to be followed by
famine, and pestilence, and trouble. The fourth one is the
pale horse and he is death. Here is a foreview, in chapter
6, of the things that followed in the other chapters, of days
of great and terrible tribulation on the earth, when the
vials and the trumpets of all of God's wrath are revealed
on the earth. Here is a day when God is going to turn
loose his wrath on the earth.

The book says that in one event one third of the population of the earth is going to be destroyed. In the past men have said that that couldn't happen. There simply was no way that one third of our population could be destroyed. Now, however, we have the instruments, we have the bombs, that could destroy great sections of the population and God's Word says it is going to happen. That is the third picture.

Antichrist

The fourth part of our puzzle reveals that there is going to arise a world ruler. While we are not concerned about it, let me remind you that Jeane Dixon says such a ruler is coming. In Daniel's vision we saw that the "prince who is to come" will make an agreement with the Jews, allowing them to resume their offerings. The prince was to be of the people who would destroy Jerusalem, so evidently the man is going to be out of the Roman Empire. That Empire is dead, but many believe it will be restored. At least a new empire will be developed in the area where the old Roman one existed. Evidently the antichrist is going to be from the Roman group.

There are many other passages about the antichrist. Let us turn to 2 Thessalonians 2:3. "Let no man deceive you by any means: for that day shall not come, except there come a falling away first, and that man of sin be revealed, the son of perdition; Who opposeth and exalteth himself above all that is called God, or that is worshipped; so that he as God sitteth in the temple of God, shewing himself that he is God" (2:3-4). Now I think that is related to what we saw earlier about the middle of the week, but let's go on and see further. Now, go down to verse 7.

"For the mystery of iniquity doth already work: only he who now letteth [hindereth] will let [will continue to hinder], until he be taken out of the way." Who is "he who now hindereth"? Apparently the reference is to the Holy Spirit, and he is going to be taken out of the way at the rapture of the saints.

"And then shall that Wicked [one] be revealed, whom the Lord shall consume with the spirit of his mouth, and shall destroy with the brightness of his coming: Even him, whose coming is after the working of Satan with all power and signs and lying wonders, And with all deceivableness of unrighteousness in them that perish; because they received not the love of the truth, that they might be saved" (vv. 8-10).

Here is a prophecy of Paul that a demon possessed man is to appear and he calls him, "the man of sin," the "son of perdition." He also is the "Wicked one" and the Lord at his coming is going to "consume" him (v. 8).

Now turn to Revelation 13. Here apparently we have the same man revealed. We see a vision of a beast rising out of the sea. "I saw a beast rise up out of the sea, having seven heads and ten horns, and upon his horns ten crowns."

This is an amazing picture that John sees and the second verse says that the dragon, that's the devil, gave him power, and we are told about the fact that he was "wounded." But look at verses 4-5. "And they worshipped the dragon who gave power unto the beast: and they worshipped the beast, saying, Who is like unto the beast? Who is able to make war with him? And there was given unto him a mouth speaking great things and blasphemies; and power was given unto him to continue forty and two months." Is that the three and a half years of which we have heard earlier?

"And he opened his mouth in blasphemy against God, to blaspheme his name, and his tabernacle, and them that dwell in heaven. And it was given unto him to make war with the saints, and to overcome them: and power was given him over all kindreds, and tongues, and nations. And all that dwell upon the earth shall worship him, whose names are not written in the [Lamb's] book of life" (vv. 6-8).

Now we do not have the time to study all the details of this picture but clearly here is a coming world leader. The devil is going to give him power. He is going to rise up in such power that the people of the world will follow him. Evidently, that will occur in the tribulation period.

Rise of Russia

Before we attempt to put these parts together, let's look at one or two other things. The biblical prophecies in Ezekiel 38 show another amazing thing — the rise of a great force to attack Israel. Many scholars believe this is Russia and her satellites.

> **And the word of the Lord came unto me, saying, Son of man, set thy face against Gog, the land of Magog, the chief prince of Meshech and Tubal, and prophesy against him, and say, Thus saith the Lord God, Behold, I am against thee, O Gog, the chief prince of Meshech and Tubal: and I will turn thee back and put hooks into thy jaws, and I will bring thee forth, and all thine army, horses and horsemen, all of them clothed with all sorts of armour, even a great company with bucklers and shields, all of them handling swords: Persia, Ethiopia, and Libya with them; all of them with shield and helmet: Gomer, and all his bands; the house of Togarmah of the north quarters (vv. 1-6).**

Other groups are named.

What does this strange prophecy mean? Who are all these people? Well, Meschech and Tubal were grandsons of Noah. Read Genesis and you will find them. It seems evident that the prophet is talking about their families, the nations which generated from these men. Where did these grandsons of Noah settle and where are their families?

Those who have studied ethnology and the movements of peoples say that that is a picture of Russia and her allies. They say that the families named moved in north of the Black Sea and across Russia. The allies named here are Persia and Ethiopia and others. These are Arabian nations. Now get the picture. Here is an enemy who is going to march against Israel in their land, and they are going to seek to destroy Israel, and it appears to be related to the same period when there is an antichrist who is the ruler. They are coming to destroy the Jewish people. In verse 8 Ezekiel says:

After many days thou shalt be visited: in the latter years thou shalt come into the land that is brought back from the sword [that is into this land of Israel that is brought back], and is gathered out of many people, against the mountains of Israel, which have been always waste: but it is brought forth out of the nations, and they shall dwell safety all of them.

The Jews are going to be there in safety and here is this horde of enemies coming in to destroy them. Ezekiel names others in verse 12 who, he says, are coming to take a spoil of these people, and "Sheba and Dedan and the merchants of Tarshish" shall join. Some believe that they will challenge the Russian horde. We are not sure, but verse 21 tells us what God is going to do: "And I will call for a sword against him throughout all my mountains, saith the Lord God; every man's sword shall be against his brother."

Look again beginning with verse 2 of chapter 39. "And I will turn thee back, and leave but the sixth part of thee, and will cause thee to come up from the north parts, and will bring thee upon the mountains of Israel: And I will smite thy bow out of thy left hand, and will cause thine arrows to fall out of thy right hand. Thou shalt fall upon the mountains of Israel." There is so much here, and all of this is part of our puzzle. Here are nations — Russia and her satellites coming to destroy Israel, but God defends his chosen people.

Tribulation Saints

We must consider another picture. The book of Revelation reveals that there are going to be some people saved during this period. This is even after the saved of this age have been taken out. The church is gone, the church age has ended, and the time of great trouble for the Jew has come. It appears that some will be saved. It is going to be a time when it will cost something to be a Christian. Now, I'm not sure whether those who already have had opportunity and have rejected Christ will have another chance if they happen to still be living. But I am sure that there are some witnesses coming, as Revelation 12 tells us, and some Jews are going to be saved and they will become witnesses.

Evidently there are going to be masses saved during this terrible period, but often it is going to be at the cost of their lives. The antichrist and his forces will kill those who dare to name the name of Jesus. There will be martyrdom and suffering. Jesus said, "Pray that you will be found worthy to escape these terrible days that are coming." The redeemed of Revelation 7:14 ff. seem to be from this period.

Superchurch

Now let us look at one last picture which is a part of our puzzle. It appears that there will arise a great superchurch but it is to be an apostate church. In other words, it will wear a name as religious but will not truly lead men to salvation.

Much of the ecumenism of our day is not based upon doctrinal truth and faithfulness to God's teachings. Many of its leaders deny that the Bible is the Word of God, and reject the truths of God's redemptive purpose. Openly the leaders say they want a great superchurch which will have political power to influence governments, effect social changes, etc. Is this the preparation for the superreligious organization which is united with the government in Revelation 13 and 17? To us, it appears to be just that.

In the last part of Revelation 13 there is a second beast. The antichrist is the first beast that rises, but there is a second beast who causes the people to bow down to the antichrist or first beast. As you follow that beast in chapter 17, he is called the great harlot. In Revelation 17:3-6 notice these words:

So he carried me away in the spirit into the wilderness: and I saw a woman sit upon a scarlet coloured beast, full of names of blasphemy, having seven heads and ten horns. And the woman was arrayed in purple and scarlet colour, and decked with gold and precious stones and pearls, having a golden cup in her hand full of abominations and filthiness of her fornication: And upon her forehead was a name written, Mystery, Babylon the Great, the mother of harlots and abominations of the earth. And I saw the woman drunken with the blood of the saints.

Now every scholar that I know studying this says here is a great superchurch.

God uses this to picture a religious organization unfaithful to him and his Word. Many believe the ecumenism of our day is getting men ready for this.

The Puzzle Assembled

Now what have we seen? We have looked at the parts of a puzzle. We have seen a week, Daniel's seventieth week. We have seen Israel back in her land during the period called this week. We have seen the desolation, the suffering of this period when the world will experience the most terrible days it ever has known. We have seen the rise of an antichrist, of a superman. We have seen the rise of nations, like Russia and others, and how they come together in a mighty battle to destroy, but we see God saying that he will destroy them and deliver Israel. We have seen some true Christians during this period and we have seen a superchurch that is working with the antichrist. There are other revelations concerning the week, but these are the main ones.

Now let's try to put it all together. The Christians are gone. Those of us who are saved will, as we said in the last chapter — at that moment when the trumpet sounds — be taken out and the world will be left without a Christian.

I imagine that after that happens some of those people who have refused to listen to the preaching of these truths, refused to listen to true Bible believing churches as they preached the way of salvation and pled with them to accept Christ, will come to the churches and say, "Those people said this was in the Bible. We had better look at our Bibles again." I imagine some of these modernistic preachers who have denied the Bible and told their people there is nothing to the second coming, or even to salvation, are going to hear people say, "Preacher, you told us that there wasn't anything to it, but look what happened. Millions of people have disappeared exactly like those preachers said." What will they say to those people? In that day perhaps some will repent and cry to God for mercy.

Meanwhile the Jew is in his own nation. In the rest of the world conditions are becoming so terrible that world leaders begin to look for a man — a superman to be the head of a world government.

Now you say, "That couldn't happen!" Are you sure? Look at what is happening in Europe, as a United States of Europe is being formed right now through the common market. Look at what is being done in the United Nations. You and I know how the United Nations has failed utterly to do what it was set up to do, but nevertheless there are many people who say we must have a world government.

World conditions will grow worse with hunger, population explosion, pestilence, trouble, war, destruction; and men are going to say, "We must have a world government and we must have a leader." A man is going to be found who is striking in his personality and ability, and who will say, "I will be your leader." The nations will turn their powers over to him and he will become the world ruler during this period. He will make an agreement with the Jews. He will say to them, "You can rebuild your Temple. You can start your sacrifices again."

But in the middle of this period, he evidently will say, "I'm going into the holy of holies. You must worship me. You Jews must stop your sacrifices. You can't talk about your Messiah any more. You have to worship me." And that's when the Jews will rebel and terrible persecution will come and then evidently this man in some way will call in the other nations and they will come, determined to destroy the Jews. They are going to attempt to wipe these people off the face of the earth.

Just when the situation looks absolutely hopeless, just in that hour when all the forces of hell seemingly have been turned loose, and when that great super apostate church is working with the antichrist and joining with him in the persecution of the Jews, and persecution of anybody who is a Christian, just at that moment something is going to happen.

Let's look at some passages which reveal what is going to happen. In the book of Daniel, Nebuchadnezzar had a dream about the kingdom and about what was going to happen and Daniel was given an interpretation.

And in the days of these kings shall the God of heaven set up a kingdom which shall never be destroyed: and the kingdom shall not be left to other people, but it shall break in pieces and consume all these kingdoms, and it shall stand for ever. Forasmuch as thou sawest that the stone was cut out of the mountain without hands, and that it brake in pieces the iron, the brass, the clay, the silver, and the gold (Dan. 2:44-45).

Here are the kingdoms of this earth, and the Lord in his return is going to destroy them.

Look at another passage. "And it shall come to pass in that day, that I will seek to destroy all the nations that come against Jerusalem. And I will pour upon the house of David, and upon the inhabitants of Jerusalem, the spirit of grace and of supplications: and they shall look upon me whom they have pierced" (Zech. 12:9-10). The Jews will see the Messiah, the one whose hands have they pierced and they shall mourn for him as one mourneth for his only son, and shall be in bitterness for him, as one that is in bitterness for his firstborn.

Now look at Zechariah 14:2:

> **For I will gather all nations against Jerusalem to battle; and the city shall be taken, and the houses rifled, and the women ravished; and half of the city shall go forth into captivity, and the residue of the people shall not be cut off from the city. Then shall the Lord go forth, and fight against those nations, as when he fought in the day of battle. And his feet shall stand in that day upon the mount of Olives, which is before Jerusalem on the east, and the mount of Olives shall cleave in the midst thereof toward the east and toward the west.**

Here is the Lord's return.

Now, once again let's turn to the book of Revelation. Remember the Lord and his church have been in the air; meanwhile here on the earth all these terrible things have been happening and toward the close of it, the Gentile nations are set up to destroy the Jews and the Bible says that is when the Lord will appear.

> **I saw heaven opened, and behold a white horse; and he that sat upon him was called Faithful and True, and in righteousness he doth judge and make war. His eyes were as a flame of fire, and on his head were many crowns; and he had a name written, that no man knew, but he himself. And he was clothed with a vesture dipped in blood: and his name is called The Word of God. And the armies which were in heaven followed him upon white horses, clothed in fine linen, white and clean. And out of**

his mouth goeth a sharp sword, that with it he should smite the nations: and he shall rule them with a rod of iron. . . . And he hath on his vesture and on his thigh a name written, King of kings, and Lord of lords. . . .

And I saw the beast, and the kings of the earth, and their armies, gathered together to make war against him that sat on the horse, and against his army. And the beast was taken, and with him the false prophet that wrought miracles before him, with which he deceived them that had received the mark of the beast, and them that worshipped his image. These both were cast alive into a lake of fire burning with brimstone (19:11-20).

So, here is the end of this period as the Lord, with his armies, comes back and delivers the people of Israel. "They look on him whom they have pierced" and they will recognize that he is the Messiah.

We will stop here and take up other events in the next chapter. I said in the beginning that this was the most difficult message to understand. I hope I have not confused you. I have tried simply to help you see the peices of the puzzle and then put them together. I have not covered the whole revelation. There is much, much more. But do not be worried if you do not understand it all. We do not have to go through it. We warn men that it is coming, but we look for the deliverance in Jesus Christ, for if we are saved, we are not going to go through the tribulation period. We shall be taken out of the world to be with our Lord, and the world, left without a Christian, will see the "abomination of desolation" when godlessness has complete control, and the Lord looses his wrath upon evil men.

5
Millennium and After

Revelation 20:6

What is going to happen after the Lord returns to the earth? This is discussed in Revelation 19 to 21, but prophecies concerning it are found in many other passages throughout the Bible. We shall refer to some of those in this chapter.

In the closing verses of Revelation 19 we see the return of the Lord in his power, the conquest of his enemies, the casting out of the beast, who is the antichrist, and the false prophet, who is the false religious leader of the tribulation period. Both are cast into the lake of fire, and those who had followed them are destroyed. These were mentioned in the preceding chapter. In Revelation 20:1-3 we find that Satan is bound. He is not yet cast into the lake of fire, but he is bound and verse 3 tells us it is for a thousand-year period, during which he will not be allowed to deceive the nations.

As we come to this thousand-year period, we are considering one of the most disputed passages in the Bible.

And he laid hold on the dragon, that old serpent, which is the Devil, and Satan, and bound him a thousand years, And cast him into the bottomless pit, and shut him up, and set a seal upon him, that he should deceive the nations no more, till the thousand years should be fulfilled: and after that he must be loosed a little season.

> And I saw thrones, and they sat upon them, and
> judgment was given unto them: and I saw the souls
> of them that were beheaded for the witness of
> Jesus, and for the word of God, and which had not
> worshipped the beast, neither his image, neither had
> received his mark upon their foreheads, or in their
> hands; and they lived and reigned with Christ a
> thousand years. But the rest of the dead lived not
> again until the thousand years were finished. This
> is the first resurrection. Blessed and holy is he that
> hath part in the first resurrection: on such the sec-
> ond death hath no power, but they shall be priests of
> God and of Christ, and shall reign with him a thou-
> sand years.
>
> And when the thousand years are expired, Satan
> shall be loosed out of his prison (20:2-7).

In these six verses, the words "thousand years" are used
six times and their use has caused one of the greatest con-
troversies of theological discussion. The issue is, will there
be a millennium? The word "millennium" is not used in the
Bible but it means a thousand years. The question is, Will
there be a thousand-year reign by the Lord and his saints
here on the earth? Will the Lord set up a literal kingdom
and sit on a literal throne here on the earth? Will Satan
actually be bound for a thousand years?

In chapter 3 we learned that there are three major
theological views concerning the Lord's return, *postmillennial, amillennial,* and *premillennial.* My conviction is that
the premillennial view is the correct one. The following
interpretation is based on that view.

Will There Be a Millennium?

Will there be a millennium? My own conviction is that

there will be a literal reign of a thousand years by the Lord Jesus Christ when he returns to the earth. Here are my reasons for holding to this conviction.

1. First of all is this passage. How else can we interpret the passage if it does not mean what it says? It says that Satan is to be bound for a thousand years. Now this doesn't say for a million years. It doesn't say for a hundred years. It doesn't say for ten thousand years. It says a thousand years. We certainly recognize that language often must be taken figuratively; yet when it is written in such a manner that there is no reason for making it figurative, then we should take it for what it says. This passage says "a thousand years," and that Satan will deceive the nations no more for a thousand years.

Then the passage presents two groups. In the first words of verse 4, John says "And I saw thrones, and they sat upon them, and judgment was given unto them." Earlier in the book, in the fourth chapter we had a vision of people sitting on the thrones, and as we studied this vision, it was made clear that these were the saints. These were the children of God of this age. Evidently, John here is seeing the Christians who have come back from heaven with the Lord, after having been taken out in the rapture, and now with him they are to rule in this world, ruling the kingdom of this world.

John also sees another group. He sees the martyrs of the tribulation period, those who had not worshiped the beast or his image, or received his mark in their foreheads, or been slain because of this, and he sees them living again. They, too, reign with the Lord for a thousand years. Then John says that the rest of the dead, the unsaved dead, lived *not* until the thousand years are ended. He calls this the first resurrection.

In the fifth chapter of his gospel John speaks of the

"resurrection of life" and "resurrection of damnation." Could this be the resurrection of life occurring a thousand years before the resurrection of the dead? That's what is said here in Revelation: "The rest of the dead lived not until the thousand years are finished."

In verse 6 we find the wondrous words, "Blessed and holy is he that hath part in the first resurrection: on such the second death hath no power, but they shall be priests of God and of Christ, and shall reign with him a thousand years."

Is there to be a millennium? This passage clearly says that there is to be one. How else can we explain it if that is not what it means? Some protest that this is the only mention of a thousand years. Suppose it is. It is mentioned this one time and the statement is very positive. It says that there will be a thousand-year reign upon the earth. If there were no other reason for believing in a thousand-year reign, we could accept it on the basis of this passage. However, this is not the only reason we believe that there will be a millennium. Let us look at some of the other reasons as revealed in the Word of God.

2. The second reason is that there is a promise that Christ shall rule from David's throne. In 2 Samuel is recorded a covenant which God made with David at the time he revealed to him that Solomon was to be allowed to build the Temple. God has said to David, in 7:13, "He shall build an house for my name and I will stablish the throne of his kingdom for ever." In verses 16-17 we find these amazing words: "And thine house and thy kingdom shall be established for ever before thee: thy throne shall be established for ever. According to all these words, and according to all this vision, so did Nathan speak unto David."

Nathan was speaking at the command of God. But you

ask, "What does this have to do with Christ reigning literally on the earth?" Let us turn to the book of Luke and read the announcement to Mary that she is to be the mother of Jesus.

"Behold, thou shalt conceive in thy womb, and bring forth a son, and shalt call his name Jesus. He shall be great, and shall be called the Son of the Highest: and the Lord God shall give unto him the throne of his father David" (1:31-32). Notice those words, "the Lord shall give unto him the throne of his father David: And he shall reign over the house of Jacob for ever, and of his kingdom there shall be no end" (v. 33).

This is not the only reference to Jesus sitting on the throne of David. In his sermon at Pentecost, Peter spoke of the throne of David and the promise which God had given him concerning it. In verse 30 he told how that God had sworn that he would raise up Christ to sit on his throne. That is on David's throne. Matthew 19:28 states, "And Jesus said unto them, Verily I say unto you, that ye which have followed me, in the regeneration when the Son of man shall sit in the throne of his glory, ye also shall sit upon twelve thrones, judging the twelve tribes of Israel."

Now may I ask you, when was this prophecy fulfilled? When did Jesus sit upon the throne of David? When did he reign over men? The Bible very clearly says that he is to sit upon the throne of David and have a kingdom. That has not yet happened. If it is to be fulfilled, it must be future.

3. There is a third reason, however, that we believe that Jesus will have a literal kingdom. Look in Daniel 7 at a prophecy of that great prophet of old.

I saw in the night visions, and, behold, one like the Son of man came with the clouds of heaven, and

came to the Ancient of days, and they brought him near before him. And there was given him dominion, and glory, and a kingdom, and all people, nations, and languages, should serve him: his dominion is an everlasting dominion, which shall not pass away, and his kingdom that which shall not be destroyed (7:13-14).

Remember the words of Isaiah when he said:

For unto us a child is born, unto us a son is given: and the government shall be upon his shoulder; and his name shall be called Wonderful, Counsellor, The mighty God, The everlasting Father, The Prince of Peace. Of the increase of his government and peace there shall be no end, upon the throne of David, and upon his kingdom, to order it, and to establish it with judgment and with justice, from henceforth even for ever. The zeal of the Lord of hosts will perform this (9:6-7).

Another passage which throws light upon this is in the eleventh chapter of the book of Revelation. "And the seventh angel sounded; and there were great voices in heaven, saying, The kingdoms of this world are become the kingdoms of our Lord, and of his Christ; and he shall reign for ever and ever" (v. 15).

Now when were these passages, these prophecies, fulfilled? When has Christ reigned over the world? When have the kingdoms of this world become the kingdoms of our Lord? Christ reigns in a spiritual kingdom today in the hearts of people, but he doesn't rule over the world, or over the kingdoms. He does not sit upon the throne of David. If these passages are to be fulfilled, it must be in the future. It must be in a kingdom which he will set up when he returns in power and glory.

4. There is another argument which must be considered. There are prophetic promises which have not yet been fulfilled and which mean nothing unless Christ literally is to have a kingdom here in this world. Look at these passages. In Isaiah 2:4 are words which tell us concerning the Lord:

The word that Isaiah the son of Amoz saw concerning Judah and Jerusalem. And it shall come to pass in the last days, that the mountain of the Lord's house shall be established in the top of the mountains, and shall be exalted above the hills; and all nations shall flow unto it. And many people shall go and say, Come ye, and let us go up the mountain of the Lord, to the house of the God of Jacob; and he will teach us of his ways, and we will walk in his paths: for out of Zion shall go forth the law, and the word of the Lord from Jerusalem. And he shall judge among the nations, and shall rebuke many people: and they shall beat their swords into plowshares, and their spears into pruninghooks: nation shall not lift up sword against nation, neither shall they learn war any more. O house of Jacob, come ye, and let us walk in the light of the Lord (vv. 1-5).

This has been considered a wonderful promise through the centuries, but when was it fulfilled? When has the law of the earth gone out from Zion which is Jerusalem? When has all the world come to Jerusalem to bow down before that nation which is exalted and to learn the ways of God? And when has the Lord judged among the nations, and when have they beat their swords into plowshares and their spears into pruning hooks? This is a dream of men, but it has not happened. If the passage is to be fulfilled, it still must be in the future.

Micah gives the same promise of the peace coming to the world and nation not lifting sword against nation and adds the words: "But they shall sit every man under his vine and under his fig tree; and none shall make them afraid: for the mouth of the Lord of hosts hath spoken it" (4:3-4).

When did this happen? It hasn't happened. A day of peace, a day of safety, has not yet come to the world.

Now consider still another word from Isaiah where we find an amazing prophecy concerning the righteousness with which the poor will be judged and the equity for the meek and how that the earth will be ruled by the rod of his mouth, and with the breath of his lips shall he slay the wicked.

"And righteousness shall be the girdle of his loins" (Isa. 11:5). Then there is a statement concerning the animal kingdom that the wolf shall dwell with the lamb and the leopard shall lie down with the kid; and the calf, and the young lion, and the fatling together; and a little child shall lead them.

And the cow and the bear shall feed; their young ones shall lie down together: and the lion shall eat straw like the ox. And the suckling child shall play on the hole of the asp, and the weaned child shall put his hand on the cockatrice's den. They shall not hurt nor destroy in all my holy mountain: for the earth shall be full of the knowledge of the Lord, as the waters cover the sea (11:7-9).

This is a wonderful passage. Here the animal kingdom is under the control of an almighty God and a change in relationships has come. Here, the knowledge of the Lord will fill the earth. Here the little children can play safely without danger. When has this happened? It has not been brought about by the preaching of the gospel. It has not been brought about by anything that has happened in the past. Then it still must be in the future.

I believe that it can come only when our Lord returns and when he sets up a literal kingdom on the earth. If these prophecies are not to be fulfilled in the future, then we do not know what they mean. If they are to be fulfilled, it evidently must happen at his return. These are passages which are meaningless unless there is a kingdom to come.

If there is to be a literal kingdom with fulfillment of these prophecies, then it must be somewhere in the future because it hasn't happened up to this time in history. Yet, the Bible says that Christ will be on the throne of David, that he will rule the whole world, that the kingdoms of this world will be under his control and that the saints will reign with him.

I am convinced that there is a millennium coming. It will be a perfect age. Satan will be bound, so sin and evil will be under control. We shall have a world without war, a world of peace, a world of righteousness, and a world of justice. It will be a world ruled by the King — the Lord Jesus Christ himself. It will be a millennium such as the world never has seen. I believe that this is the first thing that is to happen after our Lord comes back to the earth.

I could give you many more reasons for believing it, but these are enough. God doesn't tell us too much about the millennium, but he reveals enough for us to know that the Lord Jesus will reign here on this earth. The Lord is coming back to the earth with his saints. He will put down his enemies, and he will set up his kingdom.

Satan

These chapters of Revelation reveal that the devil is bound for the thousand years, and then will be "loosed for a season." Look at the first three verses of chapter 20; then verses 7-11.

And when the thousand years are expired, Satan shall be loosed out of his prison, and shall go out to deceive the nations which are in the four quarters of the earth, Gog and Magog, to gather them together to battle: the number of whom is as the sand of the sea. And they went up on the breadth of the earth, and compassed the camp of the saints about, and the beloved city: and fire came down from God out of heaven, and devoured them (vv. 7-9).

First, Satan is bound for a thousand years, and then at the end of the millennium is loosed for a season and leads a rebellion against Christ. I'm not sure that we fully understand this, except that it shows, perhaps, that merely having Christ ruling doesn't make people the children of God, and doesn't change their sinful nature. They have to be redeemed by faith. The Bible says here that when the devil is loosed, he will lead a rebellion against even the Christ who is reigning, but that rebellion quickly will be put down. This could not be redeemed people, or saints, so evidently others will be there.

Now look in verse 10: "And the devil that deceived them was cast into the lake of fire." Here is the final victory over Satan. "The devil that deceived them was cast into the lake of fire and brimstone, where the beast and the false prophet are." Remember that the beast is the antichrist. He is the ruler who rises up in opposition to God in the tribulation period, and the false prophet is the false religious leader who works with him. They both were

cast into the lake of fire at the beginning of the millennium and now the devil is cast into the lake of fire with
them to be "tormented day and night for ever and ever."

The Great White Throne Judgment

The next great event which is mentioned is the great
white throne judgment. "And I saw a great white throne,
and him that sat on it" (v. 11). Evidently this is the Lord
Jesus Christ himself, because in Acts 17 we are told that
God will judge the world by Jesus Christ. Here is Christ
on the throne, the great white throne, and it will be an
awesome sight for the Bible says "from whose face, heaven
and earth fled away."

This is the face of Christ who now is in his power and
his glory. He is not the suffering Christ who died on the
cross, but now has all the glory of heaven as the Son of
God. The Bible says that as he sits upon the throne "earth
and the heaven fled away; and there was found no place
for them." I'm not sure what that means, but it apparently
refers to the awesomeness of the hour when sinful man
has to stand before God.

Let us read on: "And I saw the dead, small and great,
stand before God; and the books were opened: and another
book was opened, which is the book of life: and the dead
were judged out of those things which were written in the
books, according to their works. And the sea gave up
the dead which were in it; and death and hell delivered up
the dead which were in them: and they were judged every
man according to their works" (vv. 12-13). Now who are
these dead that stand at the great white throne judgment?
They must be the unsaved people. All the saved people
had been raised one thousand years before. "The rest of
the dead live not until the thousand years are over," but
now, here those are raised.

Some men teach that death will "end it all." My friend, don't you believe that death ends it all! Any preacher can tell of awful experiences in being called upon to preach funerals of men and women who literally scoffed at the idea of God, and at the message of salvation, and then took their own lives "to end it all." They rejected the whole revelation and sold themselves out completely to the devil, and then tried to escape the results by death.

Death, however, does not end it all. The Bible says that every one of us is going to live forever. A thousand years from now every person who reads this will be alive. Ten thousand years from now every person still will be alive. If you are saved, you will stand at the judgment seat of Christ. If you are unsaved you will stand before God in this great white throne judgment. Judgment is certain! Eternity is certain!

The passage continues, "The books were opened." What is in those books? The Bible says men were judged from the things that were "written in the books according to their works." Does that mean God has a record of everything in your life, and in my life? That must be what it means. Jesus said that men will give account of the very words that they speak, "every idle word." This is the hour when skeletons will come out of closets.

Suppose that it was announced on television that when the morning paper comes into a community on a certain day, it will tell all the secrets of everybody in the community. I presume there would be some people that would leave town that night if it were known that on the following morning "the skeletons would come out of closets." Yet, the record is going to be opened. It is not going to be in the newspaper. God has the books. The Bible says that. God has the record and every unsaved person is going to stand there.

Now the passage says something else. The book of Life also is there. Why is the book of Life to be there if this is the judgment of lost people, and the book of Life has the names only of the saved in it? The Bible speaks about your name being written in the Lamb's book of Life. But why is this book at the judgment of the unsaved? It must be that in that day there are going to be some people who are going to say, "Lord, I was a church member on earth." Others will say, "Lord, I was as good as the church members. I lived just as decently in life as any of those people down there at that church." Then the Lord will say, "Look at the book. Is your name written here in the Lamb's book of Life?"

The only way your name can be written in the Lamb's book of Life is by your repenting of sin and believing in the Lord Jesus Christ as your Savior. Jesus said, "Rejoice because your names are written in heaven." And those names are written there when you are saved, when you have been born again, when you repent of sin and trust Jesus as your Savior. There is no other way. It makes no difference how good your works or your life. If you haven't come to Jesus alone as Savior, you cannot be saved.

Let me illustrate. Suppose you went to the president of a great railroad, with thousands of miles of lines and hundreds of millions of dollars worth of property, and you said, "I want to buy this railroad."

The president says, "Well, we might sell it to you. How much money do you have?" You reply, "Well, I don't have any money. But I'll tell you what I'm going to do. Every hour of every day the rest of my life, I'll work for you in order to earn that railroad." The president probably would call the police and say, "I have a crazy man in my office. Please come and get him out of here."

And yet I know people who say, "God, look, I want you to take my life. I want to earn my salvation. I want to earn everlasting life, the most precious thing in the world. I'll work for you the rest of my life if you will just save me." You can't earn it and I can't earn it. It was purchased on Calvary. When Christ died for our sins, he opened the way that God could save us. When we repent of sin and believe in the Lord Jesus, then our names are written in the Lamb's book of Life and we will not have to stand in this judgment.

But there will be some people who will say, "Oh, but I did all these good works and I did all this good in my life, and I lived as uprightly as that preacher did and I lived as righteously as those deacons." Will the Lord have to say, "Depart from me; I never knew you"? That is what the Bible is saying here.

Verse 15 says, "And whosoever was not found written in the book of life was cast into the lake of fire." You say, "I don't believe in hell." You had better read your Bible. The Bible has more to say about hell than it does about heaven. Somebody says, "I'll take only what Jesus said. I'm not going to take what Paul said or what John said."

Well, listen to what Jesus said. Look at Matthew 25:41. This is Jesus speaking. "Then shall he say also unto them on the left hand, Depart from me, ye cursed, into everlasting fire, prepared for the devil and his angels." That's exactly what we've just read here in Revelation. "Whosoever was not found written in the book of life was cast into the lake of fire." Jesus also said it. "Depart from me, ye cursed, into the lake of fire."

Look now at Matthew 25:46. Jesus is speaking. "And these shall go away into everlasting punishment: but the righteous into life eternal."

Let us look at Revelation 21:8: "But the fearful, and unbelieving, and the abominable, and murderers, and whoremongers, and sorcerers, and idolators, and all liars, shall have their part in the lake which burneth with fire and brimstone: which is the second death."

What is out there ahead? For the unsaved man, for the person who rejects Jesus Christ and his salvation, the Bible says there is judgment. These are awful words when the Lord says, "Depart from me I never knew you . . . into everlasting fire that was prepared for the devil."

Now I know the world does not want to believe this. But you had better believe the Bible. You won't be in eternity thirty seconds until you will know how wrong you were to reject God's Word.

The New Heaven

There is one other picture here that we need to see. In Revelation 21:1-6 we read,

And I saw a new heaven and a new earth: for the first heaven and the first earth were passed away: and there was no more sea. And I John saw the holy city, new Jerusalem, coming down from God out of her heaven, prepared as a bride adorned for her husband. And I heard a great voice out of heaven, saying, Behold, the tabernacle of God is with men [Now this is saved people. The lost have been cast into hell, but here the saved people], and he will dwell with them, and they shall be his people, and God himself shall be with them, and be their God. And God shall wipe away all tears from their eyes; and there shall be no more death, neither sorrow, nor crying, neither shall there be any more pain: for the former things are passed away. And he that sat

**upon the throne said, Behold, I make all things new.
. . . I am Alpha and Omega, the beginning and the
end.**

Beginning with verse 9 there is a description of this
wonderful city. Twelve thousand furlongs. A city four-
square. Here it is in verse 16. "And the city lieth four-
square, and the length is as large as the breadth: and he
measured the city with the reed, twelve thousand furlongs.
The length and the breadth and the height of it are equal."
Twelve thousand furlongs is about 1,500 miles. This is just
one city in the place which God is preparing. Jesus said,
"I go to prepare a place for you and if I go and prepare
a place for you, I will come again and receive you unto
myself." This one city, in this place prepared, is 1,500 miles
square, and 1,500 miles high. Read the description of this
city in the following verses. It seems difficult to find ade-
quate words to describe its beauty and glory. Then consider verse 22, "And I saw no temple therein: for the Lord
God Almighty and the Lamb are the temple of it."

Verse 27 adds, "And there shall in no wise enter into it
any thing that defileth, neither whatsoever worketh
abomination, or maketh a lie: but they which are written
in the Lamb's book of life."

Chapter 22 continues the description of the glory of
heaven. Paul once saw that glory, and after seeing it, reported, "I was caught up to the third heaven." By that
he clearly was referring to the heaven where God is, and
he said that he saw things so glorious that he could not
describe them, "things unspeakable."

I do not know all the things that God has prepared
for us in heaven, but it is going to be wonderful enough,
just to be in the presence of the Lord. Just to be away
from all things of sin and all things that hurt, and to be

with loved ones will satisfy. Somebody said, "Do you think you'll know your loved ones there?" Why, of course, we'll know our loved ones. The relationship will not be the same, but we'll know one another. The Bible says, "Ye shall know as ye are known."

For the child of God the future is glorious. We do not have to be afraid. There's nothing to fear. We do not have to be afraid of death. The sting of death has been taken away. But if the Lord comes while we are still alive, we will be caught up to be with him and move into these events that will bring us to that glorious eternal day when we will walk together for all the eternities in the heaven prepared for his own.

If you're not saved, the future has nothing for you but fear and dread and darkness. No person should want to have to stand at the great white throne judgment. He should want to go with the redeemed. As a Christian I do not want any person to be lost and cast into eternal hell. Rather I want them to walk with me through all the eternities in glory. I plead with all men to repent of sin and trust Jesus Christ for salvation now!

6

The Budding of the Trees

Matthew 24:32-36

In the preceding chapters we have seen the many events included in the wondrous prophecies concerning the second coming of our Lord. We have seen that without question this is the world's greatest coming event, and that the whole consummation of God's purposes and plans centers in it. The same question comes to our minds that came to the minds of the disciples, "When will these things be?" Our Lord has delayed his coming almost 2,000 years. Is there any reason for believing that the time for his return may be approaching? Did he give any signs by which we could know that the coming was near at hand?

Very clearly, the Scriptures teach that Christians need not be in darkness concerning the coming of the Lord. In 1 Thessalonians 5, we find these words:

> **But of the times and the seasons, brethren, ye have no need that I write unto you. For yourselves know perfectly that the day of the Lord so cometh as a thief in the night. For when they shall say, Peace and safety; then sudden destruction cometh upon them, as travail upon a woman with child; and they shall not escape. But ye, brethren, are not in darkness, that that day should overtake you as a thief. Ye are all the children of light, and the children of the day: we are not of the night, nor of darkness. Therefore let us not sleep, as do others; but let us watch and be sober (1 Thess. 5:1-6).**

This passage indicates that Christians should not be in darkness relative to the return of the Lord. Why could Paul say this? It is because there are many signs which have been given to indicate when the coming of the Lord may be near. It is these signs which we want to study in this chapter.

Our Scripture is a parable which Jesus used three times.

Now learn a parable of the fig tree; When his branch is yet tender, and putteth forth leaves, ye know that summer is nigh: So likewise ye, when ye shall see all these things, know that it is near, even at the doors. Verily I say unto you, This generation shall not pass, till all these things be fulfilled. Heaven and earth shall pass away, but my words shall not pass away. But of that day and hour knoweth no man, no, not the angels of heaven, but my Father only (Matt. 24:32-36).

After further discussing events to take place in connection with the return of the Lord, he adds "Watch therefore; for ye know not what hour your Lord doth come."

And in verse 44: "Therefore be ye also ready: for in such an hour as ye think not, the Son of man cometh."

Here is a parable which uses a very ordinary, everyday experience to present a glorious spiritual truth. Jesus says, "When the branch of the fig tree is yet tender, and putteth forth leaves you know that summer is nigh." In Luke 21:29 "and all the trees" is added. This is not a difficult parable to understand for it is an everyday experience, or at least an every year experience.

In the springtime when the trees begin to put forth the green leaves, we know that summer is near. It is a sign which cannot be mistaken. The use of the fig tree was especially appropriate since it is one of the last of the trees to put forth its leaves; so when the fig tree bursts forth in the greenness of late spring, summer is very close at hand.

Now, what is Jesus saying? The next verse tells us, "So likewise ye, when ye shall see all these things, know that it is near, even at the doors." What is our Lord talking about? In order to understand we must go back to Matthew 24:3. There we read, "And as he sat upon the mount of Olives, the disciples came unto him privately, saying, Tell us, when shall these things be? and what shall be the sign of thy coming, and of the end of the world?"

Jesus had just revealed to the disciples that the Temple was to be destroyed. As they sat upon the Mount of Olives looking toward its beautiful heights, the question naturally was in their minds, fresh from what he had just said, "Lord, when is this to happen, this destruction of the temple?" Then, remembering his words concerning his return which had been revealed to them in more than one statement, they also asked, "What shall be the sign of thy coming, and of the end of the age?"

The disciples were asking for signs. Jesus did not rebuke them, but in the message which followed he actually gave them many signs of his coming. These are not the only signs in the Bible. A number of very important ones are found in this same chapter. Others are found in Luke 21 and many others are presented in other parts of his teaching and in the teaching of other Bible writers. In his book *His Sure Return* Norman B. Harrison says that there were 110 signs of the return of the Lord named in the Bible. Whether or not we agree with that figure, we must acknowledge that there are many signs given and Jesus discusses a number of them here.

After discussing the signs he uses this parable. He reminds the disciples that they know that summer is near when trees begin to put on their leaves and then he says, "So likewise ye, when ye shall see all these things." What things? The answer is very clear. The things he has just been talking about. The signs of his coming. He says, "When ye shall see all these things, know that it is near, even at the doors." The "it," of course, is that which they asked about, his return.

In the Luke version of the story, Luke adds some further words, when he says, after giving some of the signs, "And then shall they see the Son of man coming in a cloud with power and great glory. And when these things begin to come to pass, then look up, and lift up your heads; for your redemption draweth nigh" (Luke 21:27). The very next words are the words of our parable concerning the greening of the trees.

Before we look at signs he gave, the things he says we shall be seeing, and which will cause us to know that it is near, let us look for a moment at verse 34. "Verily I say unto you, This generation shall not pass, till all these things be fulfilled."

I believe that this passage has been misinterpreted by many of the commentators. Some of them have seemed to say that the generation to which Jesus was speaking would see all of these things come to pass. Is this what Jesus was saying? Is he not rather saying that the generation which sees all of these signs will not pass away till all of the events related to his return will be fulfilled?

It seems to me that this interpretation fits into the parable far better than the interpretation which makes it mean that everything was to come to pass in the lifetime of Jesus. If that interpretation were the meaning, then the whole prophecy is meaningless since all of these things did not come to pass during his lifetime and certainly his return was not near at hand at that time. However, if the interpretation is that he is referring to the generation which sees the signs as the one that will not pass till all be fulfilled, then its meaning opens up fully in the light of this parable. He has just said that when we begin to see the signs fulfilled, know that his return is near; and then he adds that the generation which sees the signs will not pass away before all is fulfilled.

He then adds, "Heaven and earth shall pass away, but my words shall not pass away." Here is the answer to those who would deny that there is any reality to the return of the Lord or that his words have any meaning for us today. He says that his prophecies concerning his return will not pass away.

At his return the heavens and the earth shall pass away and a new heaven and a new earth will be given, but his words prophesying his return are not to fail. Let us remember that and it will help us to understand the whole scriptural teaching. His next words are: "But of that day and hour knoweth no man, no, not the angels of heaven, but my Father only." This simply means that no one can know exactly the moment when our Lord will come. We can look at the signs which he has given and can know that the coming may be near, but we cannot be dogmatic and say that it will be today or tomorrow or at a certain hour. We can only know that the coming is near and can begin to be watchful and waiting for his imminent return. By the word "imminent" we mean that it may happen at any time.

Now we are ready to look at the signs which he gave, at "The Greening of the Leaves," which were to be a sign to tell us when the coming of the Lord is near at hand. It is impossible in a brief chapter like this carefully to study all of the signs so we are first going to list a number of

them and then carefully study four signs which never have
happened before this generation. Actually some of the
signs in the longer list have not happened in the intensity
and to the degree with which they are happening today,
but for some of them there could be an interpretation
that they have happened in the past. Let us list some of
the main signs which are found in the Bible.

Some of the Signs of the Return of the Lord

1. Nations shall rise against nation and kingdom
   against kingdom (Matt. 24:7)
2. Famines (v. 7)
3. Pestilences (v. 7)
4. Earthquakes (v. 7)
5. Persecution (v. 9)
6. Apostasy (v. 10)
7. Offense and betrayal (v. 10)
8. False prophets (v. 11)
9. Iniquity shall abound (v. 12; see also 2 Tim.
   3:1 f.)
10. The preaching of the gospel to the whole world
    (v. 14)
11. Noah days (v. 38)
12. Renewal of the Roman Empire (Dan. 2; 7; Rev.
    18)
13. Rise of Russia (Ezek. 38 to 39)
14. Alliance of Russia with Arab countries (Ezek. 38)
15. Rise of dictators (Dan. 7; Rev. 18)
16. Increase of knowledge (Dan.12:4)
17. New interest in prophetic truths (Dan. 12:4)
18. Rise of ecumenical church (Rev. 17)
19. Rejection of sound doctrine Bible truth (2 Tim.
    4:3)
20. Scoffers (2 Pet. 3:3)

21. The return of the Jew to Jerusalem (Luke 21:24)
22. Signs in the sun, moon, and stars with earth distress, and the sea and the waves roaring (Luke 21:25)
23. Men's hearts failing them for looking after things coming on the earth (Luke 21:26)
24. Powers of heaven shall be shaken (Luke 21:26)

These are just a small portion of the large number of signs which could be discussed. Since it is impossible to look at all of them in one chapter, we must leave to the reader the research which he must do for himself as he takes the Scriptures we have given. Many Bible scholars believe that every one of these signs already has been fulfilled, or is being fulfilled at this very present moment. We must spend the rest of our time looking at four signs which evidently never have been fulfilled before this generation.

Four Important Signs of the Return of the Lord Which Never Had Been Fullfilled Until This Generation

1. The first sign we want to consider is that given in Matthew 24:7 which is the sign of a great and terrible world war. Jesus had just said that they would hear of wars and rumors of wars, but they were not to let that disturb them for the end was not indicated by such. Then he added that there is coming a time when a great and terrible war would come. "For nation shall rise against nation, and kingdom against kingdom." Is not this a picture of a great and terrible conflagration?

All of us are familiar with the fact that there have been wars throughout history. Indeed there have been few years in all of history when the world has had complete peace. Never, however, until the lifetime of many of us living today has the world had what could be called a World

War. There have been two such wars in this century, World War I and World War II.

Someone may speak of Caesar's legions, but history reveals that Caesar had only 400,000 men under arms. Someone else may call attention to Napoleon, but history records that Napoleon had only 750,000 armed men. World War I, however, saw 53,000,000 men under arms and World War II had over 70,000,000. Over 16,000,000 died in World War II. Fifty-three nations actually declared war. Both of these wars can be described as times when nation did rise against nation and kingdom against kingdom. Never before in history has so much of the world been involved in conflagration. Never has there been a time when war involved as great a portion of the people of the world or when there were as few areas of the world not affected by one or both of these mighty conflicts. I believe that history, carefully studied, will reveal that here is a sign which has not been fulfilled until this generation.

In this same verse we find a prophecy of famines and pestilences. These always accompany war, or follow war. Certainly there have been pestilences and famines through history, but has there ever been as much hunger and deprivation, with the accompanying pestilences, as in this generation?

Indeed, many scientists, who are students of population growth, warn us that the world is approaching a time when great sectors of the population will be starving to death. They say that hunger literally will stalk the world if the population explosion is not stopped. Moreover, this is anticipated for this generation. Some of the scientists predict that within the next ten years hunger will stalk the earth far beyond anything that ever has happened before. However, the situation even today is very serious for we are told that already 2,000,000,000 people, which is more than one half of the people on earth, are in the grip of hunger and malnutrition.

Someone has said that one third of the world is well fed, one third is under fed, and one third is starving. Estimates vary as to the number of people who are dying each day. In one record we are told that at least 12,000 are dying of starvation each day and another record estimates as high as 33,000. Estimates predict that if present world conditions continue, by the year 2000 there will be 6,000,000,000 hungry people, since, while the population will double in the next 28 years, if present growth continues, it is impossible for science to give more than a nominal growth in the production of food. Such a prophecy cannot be overlooked when we are looking at the signs, for Jesus said that there would be famine.

Another word in this verse is the word "earthquake." This may not seem important until we look at the record. Certainly there have been earthquakes throughout history, but for some reason earthquakes are increasing at an amazing rate. In the period from the year 1800 to 1896 there were six sizable earthquakes. From 1897 to 1946 this grew to an average of three each decade. In the period from 1946 to 1956 there were seven major earthquakes, and from 1956 to 1966 there were 17. This means that in the one decade, 1956 to 1966, there were more than twice as many major earthquakes as in the entire nineteenth century. This situation has continued to the present moment for there have been a number of major earthquakes in the last six years. What does this mean? I do not know, but I do know that Jesus said that before his return there would be earthquakes.

The great and terrible war, however, is the sign that we want to consider, as one which has not happened until this generation. It is the first of the four signs to which I wish to call your attention.

2. The second sign that has not happened before this generation is found in Matthew 24:14. Here we read, "And this gospel of the kingdom shall be preached in all the world for a witness unto all nations: and then shall the end come." Someone told of a great pastor in Canada who was asked by a newpaper reporter, "When will Christ come?" He replied, "I can tell you exactly when Christ is coming again." The reporter seized his pencil and paper and said, "Tell me. When?" The preacher read this verse to him and said, "Then will the end come."

This is a sign which has never been fulfilled until this generation. The great missionary movements began in the nineteenth century but have come to their full fruition in this century. For the first time missionaries have moved out to almost every corner of the earth with the gospel message. There are few tribes of people anywhere on earth that have not had some approach with the gospel.

The Bible, and portions of it, are being printed in nearly 1,500 languages, and new languages are being translated year by year. Through the use of radio and television, the message now reaches to the ends of the earth. The transistor radio has reached almost every tribe of people so that the messages flashing across the airwaves are reaching people everywhere.

Someone has said that the time now has come, through Telstar, that a man preaching before a television camera could conceivably be seen by the population on 90 percent of the earth's surface at one time.

I do not believe that the prophecy requires that every individual hear the gospel, but rather that the gospel be preached to all areas of the earth. This is happening today for the first time since Jesus spoke these words. This is a sign which has not been fulfilled until this generation.

3. One of the most important signs which has not been fulfilled until this generation is found in Luke 21:24. In the first part of the verse, Jesus is talking about how the Jews will be treated at the fall of Jerusalem with many slain and others carried away captive into all nations. And then he said, "And Jerusalem shall be trodden down of the Gentiles, until the times of the Gentiles be fulfilled." At the moment when Jesus spoke these words, Jerusalem was a Jewish city, even though they were under the Roman rule.

Here he said that they were to be driven from the city and that a long period would come when non-Jews would control it. However, he says that the day is coming when this control of the non-Jews would end. He speaks of it "until the times of the Gentiles be fulfilled." This apparently means until the time when Gentile control has been completed. If it has a reference to the Gentile age of the gospel preaching, then the meaning still could be the same, for it could mean the Gentile age is approaching its end.

From the time when Jesus spoke these words until June 1967, the Jews had never had control of Jerusalem. Some of them had lived there through the years, although there often had been persecutions against them. When they became a nation in 1948, they began to build a section of the city which was called the Jewish sector of Jerusalem. Nevertheless, they did not have control of the old city within the walls. Ancient Jerusalem was not under the control of the Jews. However, in 1967, in the amazing Six-Day War, Jerusalem came under control of the Jews and they began to rule there once again. This was happening for the first time since Jesus spoke these words nearly 2000 years ago. Now what does this mean prophetically?

The answer is given in the discussion in Luke 21.

Jesus is answering their questions concerning the destruction of the city. He tells how control is to pass from them to the Gentiles but says that the control by the Gentiles is to come to an end, and the city will be under Jewish rule once again. Then he adds some other signs in verses 25-26:

> **And there shall be signs in the sun, and in the moon, and in the stars; and upon the earth distress of nations, with perplexity; the sea and the waves roaring; men's hearts failing them for fear, and for looking after those things which are coming on the earth: for the powers of heaven shall be shaken.**

We do not know the meaning of all these words, but we do know the meaning of part of them. Whether "the signs in the sun, and in the moon, and in the stars" are figurative or literal we cannot say with certainty. "The sea and the waves roaring" may be figurative or it may be literal. In either case we could see its fulfillment today, but we do know the meaning of "distress of nations, men's hearts failing them for fear and for looking after things coming on the earth and the powers of heaven be shaken." We are seeing all of these being fulfilled at the present moment. It is the next two verses, however, which interest us. "And then shall they see the Son of man coming in a cloud with power and great glory. And when these things begin to come to pass, then look up, and lift up your heads; for your redemption draweth nigh" (vv. 27-28).

These words are spoken just two verses after Jesus talked about the Jew being in Jerusalem. He says that when the Jew is in control of Jerusalem, and when other signs are being seen, then "shall they see the Son of man coming in a cloud with power and great glory." He adds, "And when these things begin to come to pass, then look up, and lift up your heads; for your redemption draweth nigh."

The emphasis should be placed upon the word "begin." When these things "begin" to come to pass, then look up, for the coming of the Lord is near.

Any person who carefully studies what the Bible has to say about the Jews as a nation must acknowledge that this sign which Jesus gave never had been fulfilled until this generation. Never before since Jesus' day have the Jews been in control of Jerusalem, but they are there now. Does this say that the coming of the Lord is near? Jesus seems to say very clearly that it is.

Suppose, however, that the present occupation of Palestine and Jerusalem by the Jews does not last? Suppose that the Arabs or others attack them and drive them out, or even destroy the nation? It is hard to believe that this can happen, since under such circumstances, Israel would be fighting a fight unto death; but if it should happen, then it simply means that the present occupation of the area is not the fulfillment of the Bible prophecy. That prophecy cannot fail, and if the Jew is driven from the land now, he later will return.

As we understand the prophetic picture the Jew must be in the land and in Jerusalem, when some of the events related to the Lord's return come to pass. Men's interpretation of what they see happening can err; the prophetic Word will not fail.

4. Now let us look at one more sign which never has happened before, but which is happening now. Ezekiel 36 to 40 contains some amazing statements. We have examined them in an earlier chapter, but must examine them more carefully here. In chapter 36 we have a prophecy

of the Jews being returned to their land. The prophecy also tells of their conversion which is yet to come.

I will take you from among the heathen, and gather you out of all countries, and will bring you into your own land (v. 24).

And ye shall dwell in the land that I gave to your fathers; and ye shall be my people, and I will be your God (v. 28).

And the desolate land shall be tilled, whereas it lay desolate in the sight of all that passed by. And they shall say, This land that was desolate is become like the garden of Eden; and the waste and desolate and ruined cities, are become fenced, and are inhabited (vv. 34-35).

This is prophesied in Ezekiel and these very things are happening today.

Chapter 37 is the well-known prophecy of the dry bones, where in a valley of dry bones, the bones were brought together and covered with sinew, and breath came into them. It then is revealed that this is a prophecy that Israel is to come alive again as a nation (vv. 11-14). In verses 12-14 we read that God said, "O my people, I will open your graves, and cause you to come up out of your graves, and bring you into the land of Israel. And ye shall know that I am the Lord, when I have opened your graves, O my people, and brought you up out of your graves. And shall put my spirit in you, and ye shall live; and I shall place you in your land: then shall ye know that I the Lord have spoken it, and performed it, saith the Lord."

The following verses teach the prophet the same truth in the sign of "two sticks," and then verse 21 says, "Thus saith the Lord God; Behold, I will take the children of Israel from among the heathen, whither they be gone, and will gather them on every side, and bring them into their own land: And I will make them one nation in the land upon the mountains of Israel; and one king shall be king to them all; and they shall be no more two nations, neither shall they be divided into two kingdoms, any more at all."

Not all of the things in these paragraphs have yet been completely fulfilled, but they are beginning to be, for the people have been brought back to the land and are alive as a nation now. The cleansing and the making them into a new people of God is not yet done, but we are seeing a partial fulfillment which could be the beginning of the total one.

Now, having seen these two chapters, we turn to Ezekiel 38 and 39 which prophesy concerning a mighty land or nation which will move against Israel when she is back in her own land. In 38:2-6 we read:

> **Son of man, set thy face against Gog, the land of Magog, the chief prince of Meshech and Tubal, and prophesy against him, and say, Thus saith the Lord God; Behold, I am against thee, O Gog, the chief prince of Meshech and Tubal: and I will turn thee back, and put hooks into thy jaws, and I will bring thee forth, and all thine army, horses and horsemen, all of them clothed with all sorts of armour, even a great company, with bucklers and shields, all of them handling swords. Persia, Ethiopia, and Libya with them; all of them with shield and helmet: Gomer, and all his hoards; the house of Togarmah of the north quarters, and all his bands: and many people with thee.**

We are told in the ninth verse that they shall ascend like a storm against Israel. In verses following we are

told that others will join them and that they will attack
Israel, which is dwelling in safety in her own land.

Many scholars believe that this is a prophecy concerning
Russia. Now why would they say this? It is because of
some of these names. A number of them refer to peoples
who were the descendants from one of the sons of Noah.
Students of ethnology who have traced the history of those
peoples who came from their progenitor, the grandson of
Noah, know that they are people who settled in the east-
ern European area now occupied by Russia and her satellites, and many students of the Word believe that this is
a description of present-day Russia.

Here is a mighty nation which is to develop and attack
Israel. Moreover, she is to come with satellites which includes some of the Arab countries: Sheba, and Dedan,
and Persia, Cush and Put, all of which are among the
nations of the Arabs, and there are still others. This
mighty horde is to attack Israel. Beginning with 38:21 we
are told that God himself will enter the battle and will destroy them.

> **And I will call for a sword against him throughout
> all my mountains, saith the Lord God: every man's
> sword shall be against his brother. And I will plead
> against him with pestilence and with blood; and I
> will rain upon him, and upon his bands, and upon
> the many people that are with him, an overflowing
> rain, and great hailstones, fire, and brimstone.
> Thus will I magnify myself, and sanctify myself;
> and I will be known in the eyes of many nations, and
> they shall know that I am the Lord (vv. 21-23).**

In 39:1 we read, "Thus saith the Lord God; Behold,
I am against thee, O Gog, the chief prince of Meshech and
Tubal: and I will turn thee back, and leave but the sixth

part of thee, and will cause thee to come up from the
north parts, and will bring thee upon the mountains of
Israel. And I will smite thy bow out of thy left hand,
and will cause thine arrows to fall out of thy right hand.
Thou shalt fall upon the mountains of Israel, thou, and
all thy bands, and the people that is with thee: I will
give thee unto the ravenous birds of every sort, and to
the beast of the field, to be devoured."

This is not all of the passage, but it is enough to help us
see that a mighty nation is to arise against Israel and will
be destroyed by God himself. Is the stage being set for
this event? For the first time in history Russia has risen as
a mighty power and it is threatening to move into the area
where Israel now abides. Are we seeing a sign of the
coming of the Lord? If it is that, it is one which never
has happened before this present generation.

Conclusion

We have looked at some of the signs. Here are four
which are being fulfilled today which had never been fulfilled before. There are many others which also are being
fulfilled at this time. Wherever we look for a sign of the
coming of the Lord and look to see what is happening, we
find a fulfillment. What does this say to us? Look again
at the parable of Jesus. His words are very clear.

"So likewise ye, when ye shall see all these things, know
that it is near, even at the doors." We cannot be dogmatic
and say that we know that the coming of the Lord is tonight or tomorrow or within this year or next year. The
Lord may delay his coming; but again we cannot ignore
what he said. He said that when certain things were happening at the same time, then we could know that his
coming is near; that it is "at the door." This is why many
people believe that the coming of the Lord may be near

at hand. Certainly the individual is foolish who scoffs at the words and ignores them.

Jesus added that we cannot know the exact hour that our Lord will come, but he adds, "Be ready, for in such an hour as you think not, the Son of man cometh." If I ask you if you believe that Christ will come tonight or tomorrow, you probably would say no. Yet his very words are a response to that. "In such an hour as you think not, the Son of man cometh."

Knowing what we know from his Word, understanding that we as his disciples are not in darkness so that the day would overtake us as a thief, and realizing that he could come at any moment, does it not behoove us to get ready? In the next chapter we shall see how to get ready for the return of the Lord.

7
Getting Ready for the Lord's Return

2 Peter 3

A wonderful thing about the study of the second coming of our Lord is that whatever may be the position theologically, whether postmillennialist, premillennialist, amillennialist, or promillennialist, among most Christians it is not a test of fellowship. Together we all look to the coming of our Lord and when we are together with him, we'll find out which one is right. Isn't it glorious, however, to have a hope like the coming of our Lord?

In this series of studies we have had a delightful study looking at the Bible as a prophetic book, and at the coming of Christ as the center of prophecy. We have considered the great things that God has planned for us. We have considered Jesus' parable of the budding of the trees and looked at signs about us that make us believe that the coming of the Lord might be near. Now we must consider being prepared for the coming of our Lord.

This second epistle, beloved, I now write unto you; in both which I stir up your pure minds by way of remembrance: That ye may be mindful of the words which were spoken before by the holy prophets, and of the commandment of us the apostles of the Lord and Saviour: knowing this first, that there shall come in the last days scoffers, walking after their own lusts, and saying, Where is the promise of his coming? (2 Pet. 3:1-4).

Doubters

Peter said that in the last days there will be those who reject the word of the prophets. He speaks of prophecy here in this passage and of the people who reject the prophecy of God's Word and say, "Where is all of this nonsense these preachers talk about, concerning the second coming of Christ? Where is the promise of his coming?" And they add, "For since the fathers fell asleep, all things continue as they were from the beginning of the creation."

Peter speaks of them as scoffers, who say that the world goes on just like it always has. They say there is morning and there is the day and there is the evening. There is winter and there is summer. The old world just goes on and on. There are not any changes. Where is all this promise of the Lord's coming?

We have some of those scoffers today, and some of them are in pulpits. That breaks my heart, but it is true. There are some preachers who say, "Oh, I don't believe all this teaching about a second coming, saying that Jesus literally is going to come back to the earth again." Well, if they don't believe that, they just don't believe their Bibles. If you believe the Bible, you have to believe that Jesus is coming again, and when a man says, "I don't believe it," he is just saying, "I don't believe the Bible." This is true because Jesus himself said, "I will come again." Over 300 times in the New Testament, we read that Christ is coming again.

Also there are scoffers in the pews. They are people who say, "Oh, I don't believe all of that stuff about eschatology. I don't believe all that." There are scoffers in some seminaries. There are professors who say, "Oh, we don't believe all that." But when they do that, they are acknowledging they do not believe that this is the revealed divine Word of God.

They don't believe it when the Bible says in Acts 1 that two men in white apparel stood on the Mount of Olives when Jesus went back to heaven, and said, "Ye men of Galilee why stand ye gazing up into heaven? This same Jesus, which you have seen go away will come again in like manner as ye have seen him go."

These scoffers do not believe Paul when he says, "The trumpet of the Lord shall sound and the dead in Christ shall rise first." They don't believe all of the hundreds of biblical references on the Lord's return. They scoff at them. But Peter said that this was going to happen in the last days. His prophecy is being fulfilled for there are many people like this today who say, "I believe in Jesus, and I believe in the church, but I don't believe all this thing about something called the second coming."

My answer to them is just: "You are not arguing with me, you are arguing with God." The Bible says Christ is coming.

Delusion

Peter says that these scoffers are saying that everything is going on as it was, and he answers them. He shows their delusion — these doubters, these scoffers. In the fifth verse, Peter shows just how deluded they are. "For this they willingly are ignorant of, that by the word of God the heavens were of old, and the earth standing out of the water and in the water: Whereby the world that then was, being overflowed with water, perished."

Peter answers these men who say, "The world hasn't had any change. Things have gone on just like they have from creation." He says they are mistaken. He reminds them that there was a day when God dealt with this world in judgment by a flood in which the human race was destroyed except one family. He is inferring that these doubters say, "God is not dealing with the world. He is not going to do anything with men. Things will go on just like they have, for we live and we die." Peter says that it isn't so.

He said that these men who say this have *willfully* closed their eyes to a fact of history that one day in the past, God dealt with men and men had to face God. They have deluded themselves into saying, "It isn't so." But all the records show that it is so. These men were not believing. They scoffed! In his very next words Peter talks about the destiny of men.

Destiny

"But the heavens and the earth which are now, by the same word are kept in store, reserved unto fire against the day of judgment and perdition of ungodly men" (v. 7). That is the word of God that in the beginning created the earth, put the oceans in their place, and that same word of God caused the flood to come to destroy the human race. This is the same word of God about which Peter is speaking.

Peter is saying that even as God dealt with the world in the past with the flood, so today he is keeping this world; keeping it from destroying itself; keeping it from being destroyed; because the day is coming when he is going to deal with it and judge the sins of ungodly men. He discusses the destiny of this world, the judgment of men. We saw that in earlier chapters in connection with the return of our Lord.

Delay

Then Peter says something wonderful here as he reveals a delay. Why hasn't God judged the world and burned it up already? Why doesn't he just strike sinful men down and get rid of the whole sinful worldly group? Why doesn't he just wipe them all out? Peter tells why here.

"But, beloved, be not ignorant of this one thing, that one day is with the Lord as a thousand years, and a thousand years as one day" (v. 8). Now this has nothing to do with the thousand years we studied earlier. This simply reveals God's grace.

"The Lord is not slack concerning his promise, as some men count slackness; but is longsuffering to us-ward, not willing that any should perish, but that all should come to repentance" (v. 9).

God has delayed bringing men to judgment because he loves men and he just seems to be giving men a little longer period. He has delayed his coming to give men a chance to be saved, to give people an opportunity to be born again. God's judgment hasn't yet come upon men because God wants them to repent.

Peter refers to the thousand years and the one day because to God a thousand years is just a day as he gives men another opportunity to be saved. He doesn't want anybody to be lost, and yet because God has to deal with sin, because God has to deal with unrighteousness, men will be lost if they reject the redemption which he has provided. Verse 10 continues the prophetic picture. Peter now is returning to his earlier words. He has spoken of how the scoffers say, "Where is the promise of his coming?" And now he says that they fail to realize that God is going to judge the world.

Dissolution

"But the day of the Lord will come as a thief in the night" (v. 10). Evidently this is a word concerning the return of our Lord, this promised coming that the scoffers ridicule. Peter said, "The day of our Lord's coming will be like a thief in the night." Nobody is expecting him and suddenly he comes.

"In the which the heavens shall pass away with a great noise, and the elements shall melt with fervent heat, the earth also and the works that are therein shall be burned up."

I was visiting in Paducah, Kentucky on that summer day in 1945 when newspapers had the startling announcement of the dropping of the first atomic bomb. I read in the Memphis *Commercial Appeal* that amazing story of how that man had found the secret of the atom, of how a U.S. plane had flown across Hiroshima, Japan, about 8 o'clock in the morning.

The bombardier had pushed a button and a new type bomb had sped toward that great city where people were in their homes, and were in the streets on their way to work, going to school, or doing other things. It was just a warplane passing over as far as the people were concerned. Maybe there was the air warning, but nobody knew that hell was about to break loose, for in a second there was a flash brighter than anything human hands ever had made.

Then there was a noise surpassed only by the thunders of heaven itself and in a second's time tens of thousands of people were dead, and a city literally was wiped off the map. Where there had been buildings, and where there had been streets, there was nothing but smoking ruins.

As I read that story on that day, my mind went back to this passage in 2 Peter and I wondered if man had discovered the secret of the universe, and I wondered if one day, when God says, "It's enough," it would be the exploding of the atom that would burn up this old earth.

Listen to what Peter says, "The heavens shall pass away with a great noise, and the elements shall melt with fervent heat; the earth also, and the works that are therein, shall be burned up."

Sometime ago I was flying into New York City. Our plane came in over Manhattan Island. It was an unusually clear day, and I could see that great jungle of buildings on that famous island. I thought of the millions of people who lived and worked down there and I thought of the fact that one day it all would be gone. God's Word says that it all is going to be swept away.

I looked down on Chicago from a plane not too long ago and saw all those great tall buildings that are going up there and the great congestion along the lake shore. I sat there looking out of my plane window thinking, "I am seeing some of man's mighty works, but one day it's all going to be destroyed." That's what the Bible says. There will be a new heaven and a new earth and the old things will pass away. This will happen in the day of the Lord, in connection with his coming. Now we already have seen that many things will happen in connection with the coming of the Lord. It's not just one moment or one event but a number of things and one of them is this, the cleansing, the changing of the earth, and the making of a new earth.

Now look at verse 11: "Seeing then that these things shall be dissolved." Burned up, dissolved, destroyed. That's what is ahead. Now we realize that man can do it himself. We realize that man has the instruments right now, the atomic bombs, with which he could destroy the human race.

We know that right now Russia has the bombs which they could put in their submarines and destroy every great city in the United States in a matter of minutes. We know that there are bombs right now, for they have had them for years, that if a few were dropped off the coast of

California, every living thing in the United States, including man, and plant and animal life, would be dead in three days.

Khrushchev, speaking at a banquet some years ago is reported to have said, "We have the bombs that can literally take the Island of Great Britain off the map of the world." He paused a moment and then said, "And those bombs are pointed." I have recently read that men think now that Russia already has in the air, in space ships, bombs which could destroy much of the human race. Suppose some mad man presses a button?

However, I don't think God is going to allow that. I think God is reserving for himself the cleansing of this world, the removal of sin, the taking away of the works of man, and that he will rebuild the new cities, the new world. Present things are to be swept away, but something new is to come.

Discernment

Look at verse 11. Here is discernment. "Seeing then that these things shall be dissolved, what manner of persons ought ye to be?" If I know that everything is to be swept away, should I live for things that I can't keep or should I live for things that are eternal? I read about some person concerning whom they said, "Well, you know he can't take it with him, but if he can't take it with him, he won't go." But we all will go. And we can take with us only what we have given to God.

Many of us would be tempted to hold on to the possessions, to the riches, to the treasures of this world, but we are going to have to turn them all loose some of these days, because the things of this world are going to be dissolved. We can build this great civilization; we can build these great cities; but one of these days, they will be gone.

Peter reminds us that when our Lord comes in "the day of our Lord," these things of earth are going to be meaningless, worthless.

Since this is true, Peter asks, "What manner of persons ought ye to be in all holy conversation and godliness? Looking for and hasting unto the coming of the day of God, wherein the heavens, being on fire, shall be dissolved, and the elements shall melt with fervent heat? Nevertheless we, according to his promise, look for new heavens and a new earth, wherein dwelleth righteousness."

This is not a discouraging picture; not for the Christian. This is not something to make us upset and blue. No! No! Not if you have Jesus. Throughout this book we have talked about the hope which we have in Jesus Christ. Nowhere in this Bible are we told that God is trying to save this civilization.

When you find a church or preachers saying, "We are going to change civilization. We are going to remake the world," they have forgotten their commission. God isn't trying to save this old sinful world system. God is saving a people out of this world and he is going to build for them a new world, a perfect world where there will be nothing that is sinful, and nothing that is ugly, and nothing that is sad and tragic. He says here that seeing these things, that anything that we can hold on today is going to be destroyed, we ought to focus our eyes on that new heaven and new earth which is coming. "Seeing that these things are to be dissolved, what manner of person ought you to be?"

I remember an old story about a very wealthy man who lived in a wonderful mansion upon a hill. Down in the valley dwelt a poor old preacher who had little of this world's goods and owned only a very humble cottage. One day the rich man came down and sat in the cottage of his neighbor and said to the preacher, "You don't have very much, do you?"

The preacher said, "Oh, you're mistaken. You're mistaken. We are wealthy." The man looked around at the simple furniture and the signs of poverty that were everywhere evident, and he said, "Wealthy? I don't understand you. You live like this, yet you are wealthy?"

And the old preacher said, "Sir, let me ask you a question. If you knew that sometime soon you and your family were going to move across the sea and would never come back, would you be more interested in your investments here, or would you be making some investments over in Europe where you are going to live, and in securing a home and property and possessions over there?"

The rich man said, "Why certainly, if I were going to move away from this place, and if I were going to move to Europe and I knew I was going to spend all the rest of my life there, I would be interested in investing over there, and providing a place over there."

The old preacher said, "Dear sir, that is exactly what we've done. We know we are not going to live in this old world very long. We're going to move out of this old cottage one of these days, so we've sent our investments ahead. We have a mansion up in heaven. We've been putting our treasures over there. We've been concerned about where we plan to live forever." Then he said to this wealthy man, "Have you made any investments over there?" The man bowed his head and said, "I'm afraid that I've been so interested in living here that I forgot about living over there."

Diligence

Peter says here that seeing that these things are going to be dissolved; seeing that we're going to leave all these things in the world behind, what ought to be our attitude? What ought to be our concern, this world, or that new heaven and new earth?

He concludes by calling for diligence in verse 14. "Wherefore, beloved, seeing that ye look for such things, be diligent that ye may be found of him." He urges that we be diligent, not just careless about this thing. We are not to say, "Well, I may do something about my soul someday." He said be diligent, be active, do something, "that you may be found of him in peace, without spot, and blameless."

What does that mean? First, it means to be saved. Peter is saying that since this old world is not going to be your permanent abode; since this old world is going to be destroyed some of these days, you ought to be at peace with God, and the way to be at peace with God is to be saved. Are you saved? That is the important thing. That is what we have been emphasizing thoughout this book as we have talked about the second coming.

Do you want to be ready to meet Jesus Christ? to be ready for death? to be ready for his coming? to be ready for eternity? Then you must be born again.

After that, you need to live for the Lord. Peter talks here about being "spotless" and "blameless." You need to be in his church. The first command the Lord has given is that we be baptized, and when we have been baptized we are to serve him, to be good stewards. What a joy to work in the church, to use your talents for the Lord. If you can sing, sing for the Lord. If you can teach, teach for the Lord. If you can visit, visit for the Lord. There are so many things we can do as Christians to build a great church. We are to be busy for the Lord, waiting for that hour when he comes again. We are to be faithful stewards, bringing our tithes and our offerings; faithful witnesses, going out and telling friends and neighbors about Jesus; faithful Christians, living for Christ before men without shame.

Peter says, seeing that this old world is going to be swept away, "What manner of persons ought ye to be," and then he gives the word, seeing that you're looking for this, "Be diligent." Be diligent that you may be found of him in peace. If he were to come at this hour, would he find you saved? Would he find you in the church where you know he wants you to be? Would he find you busy for the Lord? If you knew he were coming tomorrow, would it change your life today and tomorrow, or could you just go on living faithfully for him every minute, just as in the past until the trumpet sounds?

If you haven't made the first start by trusting Christ, you should come to Christ today, even as you read this. If you are already saved, then you need to be in a New Testament church, faithfully serving your Lord every day.

"Therefore, be ye also ready: for in such an hour as ye think not the Son of man cometh" (Matt. 24:44).

"[He] that hath this hope in him purifieth himself" (1 John 3:3).

The King is coming! Let us live in such a way that we shall be ready to meet him joyfully, whenever that coming may be!